Welcome to

Collection Series, 1999 Edition

Celebrating the Best-Kept Secrets from Renowned Restaurants
in the Local Area and Across the Country

Since the beginning of time, a meal has been the universal activity that transcends
all languages and ethnic backgrounds. A grand meal is the canvas for celebrations of love and friendship.
A fine dining experience soothes the soul, nurtures the mind, and warms the heart.
Discover the wisdom of expert restaurateurs as you taste and enjoy their recipes in your own kitchen.

"Restaurant Secrets™" Collection Series, 1999 Edition
Great for cooking at home, dining out, or giving as a gift!

~ Happy Cooking and Fine Dining ~

Featured Restaurants...

Local Secrets

Benton's Steak & Chop House 15
Brasserie at Crown Center 65
Bristol, The 23
Californo's 19
Cascone's 61
Charlies Lodge 59
Classic Cup Cafe 41
Club 427 47
Copeland's 75
Coyote Grill 63
EBT 13
Fedora Cafe 27
Figlio's Restaurant & Bar 49
Fiorella's Jack Stack
  BBQ & Smoke Stack BBQ 53
Golden Ox 39

Grand Street Cafe 7
Guadalajara Cafe 79
Hereford House 11
Italian Gardens 73
J Gilberts Wood Smoked Meats . . . 51
Jess & Jim's Steak House 43
Johnny Cascone's Italian Restaurant 77
Jules 25
KC Masterpiece 55
Majestic Steakhouse 35
Mama Angies 85
Marina Grog & Galley 57
O'Dowd's Little Dublin 69
Paradise Grill 81
Paulo and Bill Ristorante 31
Peppercorn Duck 9

Plaza III 3
Raphael 37
Remington's 17
Soulfish Seafood Grill 45
Tatsu's 33
Tellers 83
The Roasterie 91
Timberline Steakhouse 71
Tres Hombres 87
V's Italiano Ristorante 67
Veco's Italian Restaurant 29
Winslow's City Market Barbecue . . . 89
Yahooz 21
Yia Yia's 5

Famous Secrets

Arizona: Lons at the Hermosa 51

California: Aqua 5

California: Bernard's 23

California: Erna's Elderberry House
  and Chateau du Sureau 55

California: Fio's 43

California: Five Feet 27

Florida: Chef Allen's 25

Florida: Victoria & Albert's 33

Georgia: Pano & Paul's 39

Illinois: Carlos' 29

Louisiana: Brennan's 17

Louisiana: Mr. B's 53

Massachusetts: Elephant Walk 21

Massachusetts: Salamander 15

Minnesota: Goodfellow's 47

Missouri: Cafe' Allegro 37

Missouri: Sidney Street Cafe' 45

Nevada: The Tillerman 11

New Jersey: Manor, The 41

New Jersey: Ram's Head Inn 7

New York: Four Seasons 19

New York: Tavern on the Green 13

Pennsylvania: Le Bec Fin 3

Texas: Riviera, The 49

Utah: Grappa 35

Virginia: L'Auberge Chez Francois . 31

Washington: Dahlia Lounge 9

A La Carte

Measurements & Equivalents I
Substitutions II
Wine Suggestions III

Herbs, Spices & Aromatics . . IV
Glossary V
Coach the Cook VII

 Child Friendly

 Banquet Facilities

 HeartSmart Menu

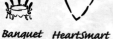 Credit Cards Accepted

 Valet Parking

   Alcohol Served

and Their Best-Kept Secrets!

Appetizers

Asian Shrimp Cocktail: The Tillerman 11
Caviar Parfait Tasting: Aqua 5
Galette de Crabe "Le Bec-Fin": Le Bec Fin 3
Lobster and Shiitake Potstickers: Dahlia Lounge 9
Phyllo Purse of Portabella Mushrooms: Ram's Head Inn . . . 7
Stuffed Artichoke Hearts: Cascone's 61

Beef, Pork & Other Meats

"East Meats West": Paradise Grill 81
Alsatian-Style Fresh Asparagus: L'Auberge Chez Francois . . 31
Baby Back Ribs: Timberline Steakhouse 71
Blackened Pork La Boucherie: Copeland's 75
Cervena Venison and Tomato-Eggplant Gratin: Riviera, The . 49
Filet Stanley: Brennan's 17
Grilled Benton's K.C. Steak: Benton's Steak & Chop House . 15
Grilled Rack of Lamb with Vegetable Strada: Cafe' Allegro . . 37
Grilled Smoked Pork Chops: Golden Ox 39
New Zealand Rack of Lamb: Lons at the Hermosa 51
Peppercorn Encrusted Kansas City Strip: Yahooz 21
Roasted Lamb and Lobster with Beurre Blanc:
   Victoria & Albert's 33
Sautéed Medallions of Beef Tenderloin: Remington's 17
Steak and Portobella "Pizza": Hereford House 11
The Majestic Rib Eye: Majestic Steakhouse 35
Twice Cooked Prime Filet: Five Feet 27
Van Noy's Steak and Scampi: Jess & Jim's Steak House 43
Veal Morel: Raphael 37
Winslow's Famous Smoked Ribs: Winslow's
   City Market Barbecue 89

Fish & Seafood

Artichoke and Mushroom Stuffed Salmon: Fedora Cafe 27
Baked Scallops: Marina Grog & Galley 57
Balsamic-Glazed Salmon: Veco's Italian Restaurant 29
Barbecued Shrimp: Mr. B's 53
Bouillabaisse de La Maison: Erna's Elderberry House
   and Chateau du Sureau 55
Calamari Fettuccine De Mare: Club 427 47
Camarones Al Chipotle: Guadalajara Cafe 79
Capellini with Shrimp: Figlio's Restaurant & Bar 49
Costolette di Tonno al Ventura: Fio's 43
Crisp Nori Tuna with Blood Orange Miso Sauce:
   Four Seasons 19
Fresh Sea Scallops: Tatsu's 33
Gravlax: Classic Cup Cafe 41

Grilled Swordfish with Fresh Basil Oil: EBT 13
Halibut en Papillote: Tellers 83
Mustard Seed Crusted Grouper with Plantains: Chef Allen's . . 25
Orange Roughy Wrapped in Potatoes: Bernard's 23
Pecan Catfish: Soulfish Seafood Grill 45
Pistachio Crusted Artic Char: Jules 25
Raw!!!: Grand Street Cafe 7
Roasted Maine Lobster over Lemon Herb Risotto:
   Pano & Paul's 39
Roulade of Dover Sole: Carlos' 29
Sea bass and Shrimp: Yia Yia's 5
Seared Ahi Tuna with Venison Ravioli: Goodfellow's 47
Seared Garlic Scaled Red Snapper: Grappa 35
Seared Tuna with Szechuan Sauce: Sidney Street Cafe' 45
Shellfish Cioppino: Bristol, The 23
Shrimp Spiedini: V's Italiano Ristorante 67
Thai-Fried Rice with Shrimp: Californo's 19

Pasta & Grains

Large Shell Pasta with Prosciutto and Peas:
   Paulo and Bill Ristorante 31
Lasagna: Italian Gardens 73

Poultry

Amber Chicken Brushetts: O'Dowd's Little Dublin 69
Chicken Fricassée with Risotto and Vegetables: Manor, The . . 41
Chicken Marsala: Johnny Cascone's Italian Restaurant 77
Chicken Marsala: Mama Angies 85
Chicken Penne Pasta: J Gilberts Wood Smoked Meats 51
Lemongrass Chicken: Elephant Walk 21
Painted Chicken Tenders: Fiorella's Jack Stack BBQ
   & Smoke Stack BBQ 53
Rosemary Roasted Chicken: Brasserie at Crown Center 65
Rotisserie Duck: Peppercorn Duck 9
Smoked Chicken: KC Masterpiece 55
Tequila Lime Chicken: Tres Hombres 87

Soups & Salads

Asian Pear Salad with Pear Glazed Scallops: Salamander . . . 15
Plaza III Steak Soup: Plaza III 3
Sam Hazen's Harvest Wild Mushroom Soup:
   Tavern on the Green 13
Tortilla Soup: Coyote Grill 63

Ahhhhh...Coffee!: The Roasterie 91
Seafood Ravioli: Charlies Lodge 59

A Message from the Restaurateurs

Come behind the closed doors of our kitchens to learn the secrets of transforming food into culinary art. Our original recipes featured in "Restaurant Secrets™" have been prepared especially for you. Each recipe includes every ingredient and preparation step, so that you can easily experience the same extraordinary results in your kitchen at home.

We hope to see you soon and look forward to hearing about your experience with these treasured recipes.

~ Wishing you many occasions of cooking and dining pleasure ~

Kansas City

Kansas City, Missouri is a sprawling metropolis on the western side of the "Show Me State" and openly shares an identity with the neighboring counties just across the state line in Kansas. Divided by the Missouri River, this city is a center for industry, culture, and transportation. Its musical history, richly filled with legendary Jazz Greats like Duke Ellington, Count Basie and Charlie "Bird" Parker, still echo strong today. Kansas City also boasts the residence and library of President Harry S. Truman, Sprint World Headquarters and the birthplace of TWA Airlines. Thanks to residents of this community, Kansas City is a "big city" with "small town" warmth.

In addition to historical and cultural gifts, Kansas City adds delicious dining to its offerings. Although best known in culinary circles for its prime-aged steaks and Bar-B-Q, as the city grows, so does the number of unique culinary experiences. Whether dining in mid-town, the suburbs, on the Plaza, or across the Kansas state line, whatever the moment requires – from festive to refined, and casual to romantic, the restaurants will provide the appropriate ambiance.

We thank the participating restaurateurs who have each graciously contributed one of their recipes to *Restaurant Secrets™*. We invite you to take this opportunity to appreciate and enjoy the signature recipes from these culinary masters. Try them at home and treat your friends and family to the entrees, then dine at one of the participating premier restaurants to compare your skills with those of the masters. Salute.

Bon appétit!

PLAZA III
The Steakhouse

4749 Pennsylvania Ave. Kansas City, MO
(816)444-6969

For over 30 years, Plaza III has reigned as one of the Midwest's finest steakhouses. When asked advice on the best place in the city to get "a real Kansas City Steak", local experts unhesitatingly give directions to Plaza III.

Set in the Country Club Plaza, the traditional cultural center of Kansas City, it's long been a fine dining destination for local and national celebrities, foreign guests and visiting dignitaries.

U.S.D.A. prime, premium aged Kansas City steaks, prime rib, chops, fresh seafood and live Maine Lobsters are all featured on the menu. Come in and see for yourself why Plaza III has earned such a sterling reputation as one of the Midwest's finest steakhouses.

A hearty steak soup filled with vegetables

Plaza III Steak Soup

PrepTime: 25 minutes
Cooking Time: 30 minutes
Servings Per Recipe: 6

1 Brown and drain ground chuck. Set aside. Pan boil onions, celery, and carrots. Set aside.

2 Melt butter in a 2-quart pan. Add the flour and mix well. Stir in water until thickened. Stir in the Accent, pepper, beef base, and tomatoes. Cook for 1 more minute, stirring constantly. Stir in the Kitchen Bouquet, all of the vegetables, and the ground chuck. Cook on medium heat for 30 minutes, stirring occasionally. Serve.

You may want to cube or small dice your ground chuck. You may also substitute the ground chuck with other steak cuts. This soup can be frozen for future use.

8 oz ground chuck

1/2 cup onions, chopped

1/2 cup celery, chopped

1/2 cup carrots, chopped

4 oz butter

1 cup flour

5 cups water

1 teaspoon Accent seasoning

1/2 teaspoon pepper

1 tablespoon beef base

1 cup tomatoes, chopped

1 1/2 teaspoons Kitchen Bouquet

1 cup mixed vegetables

Yia Yia's EuroBistro

4701 W. 119th St., Overland Park, KS
(913)345-1111

Imposing stonework, heavy beaming, wrought-iron light fixtures, and a spacious sunken dining area give Yia Yia's Eurobistro the feeling of a castle located along the rocky Mediterranean coastline.

One reviewer calls the food "exciting, attention-grabbing and loaded with vibrant flavors." Hearty eaters dote on Grilled Beef Tenderloins with a Black Pepper Gorgonzola Chianti Sauce, accompanied by Marinated Vegetable Kabobs and Mashed Potatoes or Wood-Fired Chicken with Braised Cabbage, Tuscan Beans, Pancetta, and Saffroned Onions. Others are tempted by some extraordinary pastas and oak-fired pizzas like the Four-Cheese Pizza with Oven-Dried Tomatoes, Roasted Garlic, and a Red Onion Marmalade. These pizza pies offer a welcome Mediterranean twist and are large enough to share.

Yia Yia's is located in Greater Kansas City's hottest new food/drink/entertainment/shopping area, the 119th Street corridor in suburban Johnson County.

Sautéed sea bass and shrimp with vegetable risotto and white wine, lemon and capers broth

Sea bass and Shrimp

PrepTime: 15 minutes
Cooking Time: 15 minutes
Servings Per Recipe: 4

1 **Broth:** Combine white wine, chicken stock, capers, parsley, marjoram, and lemon juice in a nonreactive bowl. Set aside.

2 **Sea Bass:** Preheat oven to 400° F. Season sea bass with salt and pepper and 2 tablespoons fresh herbs, to taste. Melt 2 tablespoons butter over medium heat in a large sauté pan. Sauté sea bass for approximately 4 minutes on each side. Add rock shrimp and broth. Finish cooking in the oven for approximately 5 minutes.

3 **Risotto:** Melt 2 tablespoons butter over medium heat in a large sauté pan. Add risotto, heavy cream, Parmesan, mixed vegetables, and artichokes. Mix well and cook until thoroughly heated.

4 **Serving:** Mound the risotto in the center of a serving platter. Top with the sea bass. Spoon the sauce and shrimp over and around the sea bass. Garnish with chopped chives.

2 tablespoons white wine

1/2 cup chicken stock

1 tablespoon capers

1/2 tablespoon parsley, finely chopped

1/2 tablespoon marjoram, finely chopped

1 tablespoon lemon juice

4 (6-ounce) sea bass filets, skinned and boned

Salt and pepper (to taste)

2 tablespoons fresh herbs, finely chopped (your choice)

4 tablespoons butter

4 oz rock shrimp

1 lb risotto, cooked

8 tablespoons heavy cream

4 oz Parmesan cheese, grated

8 baby artichokes, cooked (or quartered artichoke hearts)

8 oz mixed summer vegetables, cooked

1 tablespoon chives, chopped (for garnish)

Wild salmon and ahi tuna tartare

4740 Grand, Kansas City, MO (816)561-8000

Experience the Grand Street Cafe, one of Kansas City's best overall restaurants, consistently recognized for its eclectic regional fare and outstanding business lunches.

Grand Street Cafe is a feast for all the senses. To create the dining area's lush botanical look, actual branches of curly willow climb along the walls; providing a dramatic accent to the imported French upholstery wall covering and its oversized grapevine-like design.

The restaurant's menu reflects the same unique approach. Much of the credit goes to Executive Chef Michael Peterson, a rising star whose talent is recognized with awards won at National Competitions, and the honor of a guest chef appearance at the James Beard House in New York City.

Raw!!!

PrepTime: 30 minutes
Cooking Time: 0 minutes
Servings Per Recipe: 2-4

1 Mix raw (well chilled) salmon and tuna in a medium nonreactive bowl. Add vinegar, sesame oil, soy sauce, sugar, lemon juice, chile, salt and pepper, to taste (approximately 1 teaspoon).

2 Place onto a plate. Layer with thin sliced cream cheese. Garnish with chopped cucumber and either crisp rice paper or crackers of your choice.

4 oz wild salmon, skinned and boned, small dice

4 oz ahi tuna, skinned and boned, small dice

1 tablespoon rice wine vinegar

2 tablespoons sesame oil

1 tablespoon soy sauce

2 teaspoons sugar

1 teaspoon fresh lemon juice

1 tablespoon chile, finely chopped

Salt and pepper (to taste)

2-4 thin slices cream cheese

1/3 cup hot house seedless cucumber, finely diced (to garnish)

Crisp rice paper (optional)

Crackers (optional)

The Peppercorn Duck Club

2345 McGee, Kansas City, MO   (816)435-4199

The letters of praise for a job well done at the Peppercorn Duck Club come from all around the world. Praise for everything from the succulent rotisserie duckling to the rich sweet indulgence of the Ultra Chocolatta Bar.

The Peppercorn Duck Club's executive chef and experienced staff are highly skilled in the culinary arts and take great pride in their award-winning menu and expert personalized service.

Their dedication has not only earned the Peppercorn Duck Club its reputation as Kansas City's finest restaurant, but scores of thank yous from around the world for a distinctive dining experience.

Roasted duck seasoned with herbs served with wild rice and a raspberry sauce

Rotisserie Duck

PrepTime: 30 minutes
Cooking Time: 140 minutes
Servings Per Recipe: 2

1 **Duck:** Preheat oven to 400° F. Thoroughly combine anise, fennel, paprika, garlic, kosher salt and pepper together. Adjust the seasoning to taste. Rub the duck inside and out of the cavity breast with seasoning mixture. Place the duck in a deep ovenproof dish with a rack to keep the duck from laying in grease (you will need to drain the fat periodically so it does not accumulate). Place duck in oven; cook for 10 minutes at 400° F. Lower oven temperature to 200° F and continue cooking for 2 hours. See Chef's Hint.

2 **Raspberry Sauce:** Melt 1 tablespoon butter over medium heat in a saucepan. Add the shallots; sauté until translucent. Add raspberries, brandy and 1 1/2 cups of broth; reduce by one-third. Blend cornstarch with enough wine or water to make a slurry; then add to broth to thicken it. You may strain or keep the raspberries in, depending on your desired taste. Set aside. Keep warm.

3 **Wild Rice:** Cook the wild rice with 2 cups of stock over medium heat in a 2-quart saucepan, until kernels open up and are done. Drain any liquid that is left over. Melt 2 tablespoons butter over medium heat in a large sauté pan. Add vegetables and dried fruit; sauté until tender. Add to the rice. Season with salt and pepper, to taste.

4 **Finishing:** Preheat broiler. When the duck has slightly cooled, debone the duck by cutting in half and then remove bones except for the leg bone. Place duck halves (meat side up) under broiler. Cook until hot, then flip over and crisp up skin side. Serve with sauce and wild rice pilaf. Enjoy.

Any type of duck will be fine for this recipe. The restaurant prefers Peking duck which produces a leaner meat and is an alternative to chicken and turkey (minus the skin, of course). The duck can be roasted ahead of time up to the last step, allowing time to finish preparations for the rest of the meal.

1 teaspoon anise (available at specialty stores)

2 teaspoons fennel seed, crushed

2 teaspoons paprika

2 teaspoons garlic, crushed

2 teaspoons kosher salt

1 teaspoon pepper

1 (1 1/4-2 lb) whole duck *see chef note

3 tablespoons butter

1/4 cup shallots, chopped

1 pint fresh raspberries

2 tablespoons raspberry liqueur or brandy

3 1/2 cups duck stock or chicken broth

1/4 cup cornstarch

Red wine or water (as needed)

Salt and pepper (to taste)

4 oz wild rice

2 tablespoons carrot, diced very fine

2 tablespoons celery, diced very fine

2 tablespoons onions, diced very fine

2 oz dried apricots (or other favorite dried fruit)

★★★★ KANSAS CITY'S ORIGINAL ★★★★

HEREFORD HOUSE

EST. 1957

2 E. 20th St., Kansas City, MO
(816)842-1080

5001 Town Center Dr., Leawood, KS
(913)327-0800

Nobody in town serves a steak as tender and delicious as ours. We buy only the finest cuts of meat and allow no shortcuts in aging, cutting, or preparation. Our steaks are broiled over a hickory charcoal fire to give you that wonderful aroma and delicious flavor that can't be duplicated by any other cooking method. On October 1, 1957, Jack C. Webb began a Kansas City tradition - the Hereford House - that endures to this day. Located close to the stockyards that processed the finest corn-fed beef from Missouri, Kansas, Iowa and Nebraska, the Hereford House's popularity was natural in a city considered the major beef capital of the Midwest. "Locals" from as far away as Sedalia traveled to dine on America's finest steaks, and dinner at the Hereford House was on the itineraries of Kansas City visitors. In March 1997, the Hereford House opened a second location in the prestigious Town Center Plaza in Leawood, Kansas. Our reputation for serving the finest beef has already established us as Leawood's first choice for great steaks. We guarantee it!

A hearty appetizer...a great start to any meal

Steak and Portobella "Pizza"

PrepTime: 10 minutes
Cooking Time: 30 minutes
Servings Per Recipe: 2

1 **Marinade:** Thoroughly combine Worcestershire sauce, steak sauce, garlic powder, salt and white pepper in a container large enough to hold mushrooms.

2 **Mushrooms:** Preheat oven to 350° F. Place mushrooms in marinade. Let stand 5 minutes. Turn mushrooms over and marinate 5 minutes more. Remove mushrooms from marinade. Place on a baking sheet right side up. Bake 8-10 minutes, or until slightly tender, but still firm. Remove from oven and let cool.

3 **Steaks:** Grill or pan sear steaks as desired. Set aside.

4 **Assemble:** Turn mushrooms caps upside down (gill side up). Top caps with bleu cheese, then red onion and pepper slices. Place mushrooms back in oven. Bake until cheese melts and bubbles, about 8-10 minutes. Remove from oven.

5 **Serving:** Cut mushrooms into 4 quarters. Transfer to a plate. Sprinkle with green onions. Slice steaks into 8 pieces. Top each mushroom quarter with a slice of steak. Enjoy.

1/2 cup Worcestershire sauce

1/2 cup steak sauce

1 teaspoon garlic powder

Pinch of salt

Pinch of white pepper

2 (6-inch) large Portobella mushrooms, cleaned and stemmed

2 (4-ounce) beef tenderloin steaks

6 oz bleu cheese, crumbled

16 thin red onion slices

1 large red pepper, cut into 16 thin slices

1 green onion, chopped

Grilled swordfish over grilled vegetables drizzled with basil oil

EBT
restaurant

**1310 Carondelet Dr., Kansas City, MO
(816)942-8870**

The first thing you notice when you walk into the EBT restaurant is the elegant decor. Many of the interesting fixtures and woodworking date back to 1863.

EBT boasts a four-story atrium setting, complete with gardens, palm trees and a fountain. It is the perfect setting for fine food and elegant table settings. With its long history, EBT is an important landmark for Kansas City and has won many awards throughout the years, a testimony to its excellence.

Tableside preparations of Caesar Salads, Flaming Pepper Steaks and Bananas Foster are a favorite tradition and keep patrons coming back for more. EBT is truly one of the finest restaurants in Kansas City.

Grilled Swordfish with Fresh Basil Oil

PrepTime: 25 minutes
Cooking Time: 7-8 minutes
Servings Per Recipe: 4

1 **Basil Oil:** Blend 1 cup olive oil and basil in a blender until smooth. Set aside.

2 **Vegetables:** Toss all vegetables in a large bowl with 1/2 cup olive oil. Season with salt and pepper, to taste. Grill vegetables 2 minutes on each side.

3 **Swordfish:** Lightly oil and pepper swordfish on both sides. Grill 3 1/2-minutes on each side.

4 **Serving:** Arrange vegetables by alternating colors around center of each plate. Place swordfish over vegetables. Drizzle vegetables and swordfish with basil oil. Serve with lemon wedges.

4 oz fresh basil leaves

1 1/2 cups olive oil + additional

2 red bell peppers, seeded and quartered

2 yellow bell peppers, seeded and quartered

2 green bell peppers, seeded and cut into quarters

4 Roma tomatoes, halved

8 asparagus spears, ends snapped off

2 medium portabella mushrooms, halved

4 green onions

2 yellow squash, quartered

Salt and pepper (to taste)

4 (7 to 8-ounce) Swordfish filets or steaks

1 lemon, cut into wedges

Benton's
steak & chop house

Westin Crown Center, Kansas City, MO
(816)391-4460

At Benton's Steak & Chop House atop the Westin Crown Center, you'll not only experience a breathtaking view of the city, you'll feast on the best steak Kansas City has to offer.

Select from a dinner menu of steaks and chops, as well as ocean-fresh seafood, all charbroiled to perfection and brought sizzling from the grill.

The restaurant decor is centered around a charming display of original works by Missouri's legendary artist, Thomas Hart Benton. Benton's also has a spectacular brunch on Sundays.

Kansas City steaks grilled to perfection with dauphinoise potatoes

Grilled Benton's K.C. Steak

PrepTime: 20 minutes
Cooking Time: 210 minutes
Servings Per Recipe: 8

1 **Dauphinoise Potatoes:** Preheat oven to 225° F. Combine the two cheeses in a bowl. In a large bowl, combine the half and half, eggs, salt, pepper, garlic, nutmeg. Mix well. Add three-fourths of the cheese mixture. Slice the potatoes very thin using a food processor or mandoline. Add to the custard mixture. Place into a large ovenproof casserole dish. Sprinkle with remaining cheese. Bake for 3 1/2 hours or until an inserted sharp knife comes out clean.

2 **Steaks:** Preheat an open flame grill with hickory chips. Season steaks with seasoning salt. Grill steaks evenly on both sides, approximately 5-7 minutes on each side or until desired doneness. Serve with potatoes and enjoy.

4 cups half and half

8 large eggs

1 tablespoon salt

1/2 tablespoon white pepper

1/2 tablespoon garlic, chopped

1/2 tablespoon ground nutmeg

1/2 lb Gruyere cheese

1/2 lb Swiss cheese

2 1/2 lb potatoes, peeled

8 (10-ounce) choice Kansas City steaks (3/4-inch cut)

4 tablespoon seasoning salt

Served with a Madeira wine mushroom demi-glace

Remington's
Steak & Seafood Grill

9103 E. 39th St., Kansas City, MO
(816)737-4760

Remington's Steak & Seafood Grill features a contemporary twist on classic American West cuisine such as certified angus beef steaks and fresh seafood are prepared to perfection on the hardwood grill. Choose from a delicious selection of creative desserts to top off your meal.

Remington's has proudly won numerous Wine Spectator awards for their extensive wine menu and special reserve list. The atmosphere is casual, yet elegant and the dining room features light jazz nightly. It is the perfect place to meet friends for a night out or for the fabulous Sunday Brunch.

Sautéed Medallions of Beef Tenderloin

PrepTime: 15 minutes
Cooking Time: 25-30 minutes
Servings Per Recipe: 2

1 **Tabasco Onions:** Heat a fryer with oil. Place onions in a medium bowl. Add a few drops of Tabasco, and sprinkle with paprika. Mix well. Dredge in seasoned flour, shake off excess flour. Reserve remaining flour for tenderloins. Fry until golden brown. Place on paper towel to absorb any excess oil.

2 Heat oil over medium-high heat in a large sauté pan. Dredge medallions in seasoned flour. Add medallions to pan and brown on both sides; remove and keep warm. Add shallots, garlic, mushrooms, and cracked black pepper to pan and sauté until mushrooms are tender. Add wine; reduce by half. Add demi-glace; return medallions to pan. Cook to desired doneness in sauce.

3 **Serving:** Divide onions among plates. Top with 2 medallions each. Ladle sauce equally over medallions. Serve with fresh vegetables of choice.

1 yellow onion, peeled and very thinly sliced

Few drops Tabasco sauce

1/2 teaspoon paprika

1 cup seasoned flour (flour seasoned with salt and pepper, to taste)

4 (5-ounce) beef tenderloin medallions

2 tablespoons oil

2 tablespoons shallots, chopped

1 tablespoon garlic, chopped

2 oz wild mushrooms (shiitake, Portabella, chanterelle)

1 tablespoon cracked black pepper

1/2 cup Madeira wine

2 oz wild mushrooms (shiitake, Portabella, chanterelle)

★ ★ ★ ★
CALIFORNOS
WESTPORT

4124 Pennsylvania, Kansas City, MO
(816)531-7878

Californo's Westport is a French-styled open-air sidewalk cafe. It is a bistro complete with a steak menu, a four-level cedar deck opened seasonally with bar and fireplace, and Four Star dining reviews from the Kansas City Star and Star Magazine.

Opened in 1988 by Chef Brenda Burns and her business manager husband, Terry, Californo's is located in the heart of Kansas City's entertainment district, adjacent to Westport's historic Trolley Barn.

Californo's Westport is the perfect place for a romantic night on the town or to entertain for business.

Sautéed shrimp with a vegetable fried rice

Thai-Fried Rice with Shrimp

PrepTime: 30 minutes
Cooking Time: 15 minutes
Servings Per Recipe: 4

1 Heat a wok over high heat with 1 tablespoon sesame oil. When hot add shrimp. Sauté until cooked through. Set aside.

2 Add 2 tablespoons sesame oil, ginger, garlic, and chili paste to wok. Sauté 2-3 minutes. Add sliced carrots, broccoli, cauliflower florettes, red pepper, yellow squash, and zucchini. Sauté 2-3 minutes. Push mixture to sides, exposing center of wok. Add egg in center and scramble. Add jasmine rice and combine ingredients in wok. Add fish oil, to taste.

3 Place rice onto platter and top with shrimp. Top with scallions, peanuts, black and white sesame seeds. Garnish perimeter of plate with julienned carrots and leeks mixed together.

4 cups cooked jasmine rice

3 tablespoons sesame oil

1 lb medium shrimp, peeled and deveined

1 tablespoon fresh ginger, grated

2 teaspoons fresh garlic, finely chopped

1-4 teaspoons chili paste (depends upon desired hotness)

1 cup carrots, thinly sliced

1 cup broccoli florettes

1 cup cauliflower florettes

1 cup red bell peppers, julienned

1 cup yellow squash, julienned

1 cup green zucchini, julienned

3 eggs, beaten

1/4 cup fish oil

1 scallion, chopped (to garnish)

Crushed peanuts (to garnish)

Black sesame seeds (to garnish)

White sesame seeds (to garnish)

1 carrot, julienned (to garnish)

1 leek, white part only, julienned (to garnish)

Kansas City's signature steak paired with a tasty bourbon peppercorn sauce

4701 Town Center Dr., Leawood, KS
(913)451-8888

Plan on kicking back and relaxing at Yahooz, contemporary cowboy cuisine at its finest. Voted "Best New Restaurant - 1998" by Ingram's magazine, Yahooz offers a spectacular ranch setting highlighted by three fireplaces, blue spruce lodge poles and fantastic murals of cowboy life.

Begin your culinary journey with a "trailstarter" like the Barbecued Shrimp with Cheddar Cheese Grits or the Beef Tenderloin Tostada. Enjoy absolutely delectable steaks, tasty and tender pork chops, fresh fish, pasta, chicken and intriguing salads from Yahooz's award-winning menu.

Looking for a lunch that can't be beat? Try Yahooz for its wildly popular Chicken Fried Steak or Best in the West Enchilada Platter. Whenever you saddle up and head to Yahooz, be sure to save room for divine desserts prepared daily by our in-house pastry chef. Don't forget to whet your whistle with a hand-shaken margarita or selection from our masterful wine list.

Peppercorn Encrusted Kansas City Strip

PrepTime: 15 minutes
Cooking Time: 30 minutes
Servings Per Recipe: 4

1 **Roasted Mushroom:** Preheat oven to 350° F. Combine butter and mushrooms in an oven-safe pan; cook for 30 minutes. Separate juices and mushrooms. Reserve both for sauce.

2 **Steak:** Mix cracked black peppercorns and salt together. Rub on both sides of steaks. Grill over hot fire to desired temperature.

3 **Sauce:** Combine bourbon, beef bouillon, green peppercorns, mushroom juice, and Dijon in a small sauce pan. Bring to a simmer over medium heat and reduce by half. Add mushrooms and cream and reduce by half. Season with salt and pepper, to taste. Serve over prepared steaks. Enjoy!

2 tablespoons butter

4 oz variety of mushrooms

1 tablespoon cracked black peppercorn

2 teaspoons kosher salt

4 Kansas City strip steaks, trimmed

2 tablespoons bourbon

1/2 cup beef bouillon (broth)

2 teaspoons cracked green peppercorns

2 tablespoons mushroom juice (see recipe)

2 teaspoons Dijon mustard

1/2 cup roasted mushroom blend (see recipe)

1/2 cup heavy cream

5400 W. 119th St., Overland Park, KS
(913)663-5777

From the magnificent stained-glass domed ceiling to the seafood flown in fresh daily from as far away as Australia, everything about The Bristol in Kansas City is impressive.

For instance, a mesquite grill adds a flavorful dimension to not only the ambiance, but the menu. An oyster bar and exhibition kitchen let patrons see the action. Alcoves for dining allows for privacy, and of course there's the seafood.

Oysters and crab cakes are all the rage, but there's a lot more than just great seafood at The Bristol. Guests also rave about the fine cuts of beef, tantalizing chicken and splendid pasta entrees - not to mention the famous drop biscuits that arrive irresistibly hot out of the oven.

A combination of fish and seafood cooked in a marinara sauce

Shellfish Cioppino

PrepTime: 25 minutes
Cooking Time: 30 minutes
Servings Per Recipe: 4

1 **Sauce Base:** In heavy 2-quart sauce pan, heat oil and garlic, over medium heat, until lightly browned. Add tomatoes, marinara sauce, water, and wine. Simmer for approximately 15 minutes. Dissolve cornstarch in the clam juice. Stir into sauce, along with the herbs and salt. Bring up to a light boil and simmer for 5 minutes. Stir in pepper and lemon rind.

2 **Cioppino:** In a large sauté pan or fry pan, heat white wine over medium-high heat. Add fish, scallops, shrimp, and mussels. Poach until fish is cooked half way and wine is reduced by half. Add prepared base sauce and remaining seafood. Simmer until mussels are opened and all the seafood is cooked and lobster is hot.

3 **Serving:** In a large soup bowl sprinkle with parsley and serve along with sourdough bread.

This dish can also be served over linguini.

For the Sauce Base:

1 oz olive oil

3 tablespoons garlic, peeled and minced

2 cups canned tomatoes with juice, diced

1 1/2 cups marinara sauce

1 cup water

1 cup red wine

1 cup clam juice

1 tablespoon cornstarch

1 tablespoon dried basil leaves

1/2 tablespoon oregano

1/2 teaspoon salt

1/4 teaspoon coarse ground black pepper

1/2 tablespoon grated lemon rind

For the Cioppino:

1 cup dry white wine

12 tablespoons firm fresh fish (such as grouper, snapper, or sea bass), cut into 1 inch cubes

8-12 medium scallops

12 each medium shrimp, peeled and deveined

16 mussels, cleaned

6 oz calamari, cut into 1 1/2 inch strips

4 lobster claws or 2 crab claws (steamed or broiled ahead of time)

4 teaspoons fresh parsley, chopped (to garnish)

Sourdough bread

JULES'®
SEAFOOD ON THE PLAZA

4740 Jefferson, Kansas City, MO
(816)561-4004

Jules is seafood sophistication located on the beautiful County Club Plaza and it sparkles with creativity.

Chef David Lynch prepares his innovative and progressive dishes using only the season's freshest catches flown in daily from around the world.

A visually stunning restaurant, it boasts a raw oyster bar, fantastic Sunday Brunch, extensive wine list, and the occasional Mermaid visit. Jules is the sea and seafood lovers' dream.

AAA Four Diamond Award winner in '97 and '98.

Sautéed char encrusted with pistachios
and topped with blueberries

Pistachio Crusted Arctic Char

PrepTime: 15 minutes
Cooking Time: 15 minutes
Servings Per Recipe: 2

1 Season char with salt and pepper. Lightly bread with finely chopped pistachios. Heat a large skillet over medium heat. Add oil, enough to cover bottom of pan. Place char, belly side down, in skillet. Sauté until golden brown. Turn over. Lower heat. Cook until flesh is slightly firm.

2 Place char onto serving plates. Top with fresh blueberries. Serve with your favorite rice and fresh vegetable.

Char can be substituted with salmon (baby coho) or fresh ozark trout.

2 (8-ounce) fresh Arctic char filets, boned and skinned

Salt and pepper (to taste)

1 cup pistachios, finely chopped

2 tablespoons olive oil

1/2 cup fresh blueberries

A warming entree with a light sauce

fedora
CAFE

T.M.

210 W. 47th St., Kansas City, MO
(816)561-6565

When planning the menus for the award-winning Fedora Cafe, Executive Chef Chris Deaton takes his cue from nature. This American bistro specializes in dishes prepared from available seasonal fruits, vegetables, fish and meats.

Proclaimed one of the most romantic restaurants in Kansas City, Fedora also features live jazz during the evening hours and offers attentive service.

After your meal, enjoy a chilled martini, or glass of single malt Scotch and a premium cigar at the bar. No matter what your taste, Fedora Cafe is always in season.

Artichoke and Mushroom Stuffed Salmon

PrepTime: 80 minutes
Cooking Time: 20 minutes
Servings Per Recipe: 4

1 **Marinade:** Thoroughly mix together dry vermouth, 2 tablespoons lemon juice, lemon pepper, garlic powder, parsley, salad oil and cracked black pepper in a nonreactive bowl. Refrigerate. (This can be made ahead of time.)

2 **Stuffing:** Combine artichoke hearts, mushrooms, Parmesan cheese, 1 1/2 tablespoons marinade, and a pinch of nutmeg in a mixing bowl. Mix well. Season with salt and pepper. Refrigerate 1 hour.

3 **Salmon:** Preheat oven to 350° F. Cut a cross on top of salmon filet three-fourths of the way down. Divide stuffing mixture into 4 equal parts, then stuff each filet. Season with salt and pepper. Heat a 12-inch ovenproof nonstick skillet. Add olive oil. Sear stuffing side of salmon until golden brown. Turn salmon over. Place skillet in oven for 10 minutes, or until desired doneness. Remove salmon from skillet; keep warm.

4 **Sauce:** Return skillet to stove over medium heat. Add capers, red onions, spinach, and tomatoes. Sauté for 1 minute. Deglaze with white wine and 1 teaspoon lemon juice. Reduce by half. Remove from heat. Whisk in butter until incorporated. Season with salt and pepper.

5 **Serving:** Place fish onto plate and cover with sauce. Serve with a rice pilaf or couscous. Enjoy.

Marinade is all purpose. Use extra marinade for grilling, sautéing or other uses.

1/2 cup dry vermouth

2 1/2 tablespoon fresh lemon juice

3 teaspoons lemon pepper

1/2 teaspoon garlic powder

1/4 cup parsley, chopped

1 cup salad oil

1/2 teaspoon cracked black pepper

1 cup artichoke hearts, quartered

1/2 cup button mushrooms, quartered

3 tablespoons Parmesan cheese, grated

Pinch of nutmeg

Salt and pepper (to taste)

4 (8-ounce) salmon filets, boned and skinned

2 tablespoons olive oil

1 tablespoon capers

1 tablespoon red onion, chopped

2 tablespoons fresh spinach, chopped

2 tablespoons tomatoes, diced

1/4 cup white wine

2 tablespoons butter

VĒCO

1803 W. 39th St., Kansas City, MO
(816)931-2101

Veco's Italian Restaurant is a casual, comfortable Italian-style bistro serving selections of truly unique entrees from both the northern and southern regions of Italy.

Veco's takes pride in specializing in dining that manages to be trendy and intimate at once, with an emphasis on fantastic service.

It's the kind of restaurant that serves excellent food but doesn't expect you to get too dressed up. Just relax, leave your keys with the valet and sit back for some truly fantastic Italian food.

Grilled filet of salmon with a balsamic glaze

Balsamic-Glazed Salmon

PrepTime: 10 minutes
Cooking Time: 8 minutes
Servings Per Recipe: 4

1 **Glaze:** In a small sauce pan over medium heat, cook the garlic in the olive oil until it is soft. Do not brown. Add honey, Dijon mustard, balsamic vinegar, salt and black pepper, to taste. Stir until combined. Simmer until thickened, about 3-5 minutes; sauce should coat the back of a spoon. Set aside; keep warm.

2 **Salmon:** Coat salmon filets with oil and season with salt and black pepper. Grill to degree of desired doneness.

3 **Serving:** Place salmon filets on plates. Spoon balsamic glaze evenly over the salmon. Garnish with fresh basil if desired. For accompaniments use orzo or risotto and fresh grilled asparagus.

Glaze can be made ahead of time and refrigerated. Reheat before serving.

1 tablespoon olive oil

2 large cloves garlic, sliced paper thin

1 tablespoon honey

1 tablespoon Dijon mustard

1/3 cup balsamic vinegar

Salt (to taste)

Freshly ground black pepper (to taste)

4 (6-ounce) salmon filets, skinned and boned

2 tablespoons fresh basil, julienned

Large pasta shells tossed with prosciutto, peas and mushrooms

ristorante

16501 Midland Dr., Shawnee, KS
(913)962-9900

It is the intention of the creators of Paulo and Bill Ristorante that it serve as a model for the next generation of Italian restaurants in America.

Judging by some recent accolades, Paulo and Bill Ristorante may well be on their way in that endeavor even though they've only been around a few years. Winner of the 1996 Silver Ladle Award for Best New Restaurant, they were also instrumental in PB & J's elevation to the 1996 Concept Creators list published by Restaurants & Institutions Magazine.

Paulo and Bill's expertise lies in creating exciting new twists on both regional Italian and traditional Italian-American dishes. The previously featured bowtie chicken pasta and the mountain sized lasagna are just two of the many highly recognized items they invite you to try.

Large Shell Pasta with Prosciutto and Peas

PrepTime: 17 minutes
Cooking Time: 30 minutes
Servings Per Recipe: 6

1 Heat a large skillet over medium heat. When hot add oil, ham, peas, and mushrooms. Sauté about 2 minutes. Stir in cream and cheese. Cook until cheese has melted, stirring frequently. Add the cooked shell pasta to the pan. Toss until sauce begins to thicken. Season with salt and pepper, to taste. Serve.

2 tablespoons olive oil

8 oz prosciutto ham, julienned

1 cup sugar snap peas, cut into thirds

1 cup crimini mushrooms, sliced

2 cups heavy cream

4 oz fresh Parmesan cheese, grated

8 cups shell pasta, cooked

Salt and pepper (to taste)

Tatsu's
FRENCH RESTAURANT

4603 W. 90th St., Prairie Village, KS
(913)383-9801

Classic French cuisine best describes the award-winning dishes prepared at Tatsu's, a simple yet elegant restaurant that has quietly served beloved French standards for nearly two decades.

With a menu offering delicacies like ocean fresh scallops and salmon, Chef Tatsu Avais never disappoints his customers. His specialties include Beef Bourguignon, Veal Normande, Chicken Herbs and a popular vegetarian dish specially created by Tatsu.

Genuine and tasteful, the ambiance at Tatsu's is made even more inviting by the fresh flowers placed daily on the tables. Located in a quiet but professional area, Tatsu's French Restaurant is the real thing.

Sautéed scallops and mushrooms in a light sauce

Fresh Sea Scallops

PrepTime: 5 minutes
Cooking Time: 3 minutes
Servings Per Recipe: 2

1 Season scallops with salt and pepper, to taste. Dust with flour. Heat oil over high heat in a skillet. Add scallops. Sear on both sides. Add mushrooms. Cook until tender.

2 Remove scallops and mushrooms from skillet. Set aside. Add lemon, butter, and white wine to pan. Mix well.

3 Place scallops and mushrooms onto plates. Pour sauce over and serve.

12 oz sea scallops, cleaned and pat dry

Salt and pepper (to taste)

1/4 cup flour

2 teaspoons oil

8 oz fresh mushrooms

2 tablespoons fresh lemon juice

1 oz butter

2 tablespoons white wine

Grilled rib eye with a roasted red pepper sauce

THE MAJESTIC Steakhouse

931 Broadway, Kansas City, MO (816)471-8484

The new Majestic Steakhouse takes its name directly from the old Kansas City landmark with the same name. Housed in a restored turn-of-the century garment district building, dark old woods, high stamped-tin ceilings and leaded glass light fixtures add a certain visual flavor to your dining experience.

Steaks at the Majestic are the main focus with Roast Prime Rib sold by the thickness of the cut.

The Grilled Salmon Filet and the Fettucine Alfredo with Grilled Chicken are also highly rated and are especially recommended. You will have no difficulty choosing an entree. Majestic's wine list, with over 700 wines, will complement any of them. .

The Majestic Rib Eye

PrepTime: 20 minutes
Cooking Time: 15 minutes
Servings Per Recipe: 6

1 **Sauce:** Combine sour cream, horseradish, roasted peppers, Worcestershire, Tabasco, black pepper, and salt in a mixing bowl until smooth. Set aside.

2 **Steaks:** Heat a grill. Brush with olive oil. Season steaks with salt and pepper, to taste. Grill on both sides to desired doneness. Serve with sauce. Enjoy!

Roasted red peppers may be purchased or prepared at home. Prepare peppers by grilling or roasting 6 red bell peppers until charcoal black. Chill for 5 minutes in ice water. Remove skin, stem, and seeds and puree in blender or food processor.

1 cup sour cream

1/3 cup prepared horseradish, minced

1/4 cup roasted red peppers, pureed (see Chef Hint)

2 tablespoons Worcestershire sauce

4 drops Tabasco sauce

1 1/2 oz cracked black pepper

1/2 oz salt

Olive oil (as needed)

6 (12-ounce) Rib eye steaks

Salt and pepper (to taste)

Scalloppine of veal with a dry vermouth and morel mushroom sauce

The Raphael Restaurant

325 Ward Parkway, Kansas City, MO
(816)756-3800

Elegant Old-World charm and the ambiance of a real European restaurant make the Raphael a favorite dining destination.

Voted the "Most Romantic" restaurant and "Best Kept Secret" by Ingram's magazine, Raphael's intimate dining room attracts its share of first dates and special occasions.

But most folks find Raphael's award-winning menu reason enough to stop in anytime for fine dining. The featured recipe, Veal Morel, has been a signature dish at the Raphael for years. The melt-in-your-mouth tenderness of the Veal Scalloppine paired with the dry vermouth sauce and earthy morel mushrooms make this dish a true favorite.

If you are in love or just love excellent food, you will love the Raphael.

Veal Morel

PrepTime: 15 minutes
Cooking Time: 10 minutes
Servings Per Recipe: 2

1 Heat a small skillet on medium high heat. Add clarified butter. Dredge the veal in the seasoned flour and shake off the excess. Add to the hot butter. Brown veal well, turn, and brown the second side. Add the morel mushrooms, shallots, and garlic. Cook for 2-3 minutes. Deglaze the pan with the dry vermouth. Add the wine, lemon juice, heavy cream, brown sauce, butter, and salt and pepper, to taste. Return to the heat and cook until the liquid has reduced to a thick sauce.

2 Place the veal on a dinner plate with the morel mushrooms on top. Spoon the sauce over top. Serve with mashed potatoes or rice and fresh vegetables.

1 tablespoon clarified butter

4 (approximately 2 1/2-ounce) veal scalloppine

Flour, seasoned with salt and pepper (to taste)

6 large morel mushrooms, fresh or dried (soaked in water)

2 teaspoons shallots, minced

2 teaspoons garlic, minced

4 tablespoons dry vermouth

4 tablespoons white wine

2 tablespoons lemon juice

1 cup heavy cream

1 cup brown sauce

2 teaspoons butter

Salt and pepper (to taste)

This is the way pork chops should taste

the GOLDEN OX

1600 Genessee, Kansas City, MO
(816)842-2866

The Golden Ox is Kansas City's oldest and most famous steakhouse. In fact, this year the Golden Ox celebrates its 50th anniversary, and can safely say they've served more steaks thus far than any other Kansas City restaurant. That's a lot of steaks.

Still located in the old Stockyard District, the Golden Ox proudly displays their heritage with pictures throughout the restaurant. You'll see pictures of the "old days," when the stockyards were in operation, and pictures of the flood of 1952 and the great fire of 1917.

Come enjoy an excellent meal at Kansas City's oldest and most famous steakhouse.

Grilled Smoked Pork Chops

PrepTime: 5 minutes
Cooking Time: 15 minutes
Servings Per Recipe: 4

1 **Smoking of Chops:** Smoke the center cut pork chops over the charcoal and hickory hardwood chunks. This will give the chops a very nice smoky hickory flavor. After the chops have been smoked, allow the chops to cool and place in refrigerator until used for grilling.

2 **Grilling of Smoked Pork Chops:** Prepare hickory hardwood charcoal for grilling. Rub the smoked pork chops with olive oil, salt and pepper, and minced garlic. Grill smoked pork chops 4-6 minutes over a low to medium heat.

4 (1-pound) center cut pork chops

Virgin olive oil (as needed)

1 teaspoon salt

1 teaspoon pepper

1 clove garlic, peeled and minced

Smoking of Chops:

Hickory Hardwood Charcoal

Hickory Hardwood chunks (soaked in water for 2 hours)

CLASSIC CUP CAFE
PLAZA

301 W. 47th St., Kansas City, MO
(816)753-1840

At the Classic Cup Cafe on the Country Club Plaza, Chef Michael Turner is serving up what he calls the "New American Comfort" foods.

Consistent winners of a Best Outdoor Cafe Award, the Classic Cup offers breakfast, lunch and dinner seven days a week while an on-site bakery provides the irresistible aroma of fresh baked breads and delectable desserts.

Try a few with their famous selection of coffees. Their wine list is a venerable recipient of Wine Spectator Magazine's Award of Excellence.

Salmon marinated in dill and aquavit

Gravlax

PrepTime: 30 minutes
Cooking Time: 0 minutes
Servings Per Recipe: 4-6

1 **The salmon must marinate for 48-72 hours.** Place one-half of the fish, skin side down, in a deep glass or stainless steel container. Spread the dill over the salmon. Sprinkle the remaining dry ingredients over the fish. Pour the aquavit over all. Top with the other half of the salmon skin side up. Cover with plastic wrap and weigh down with another container and a 5-pound weight (a brick or can of juice work well!). Refrigerate for 48-72 hours, turning the salmon and basting every 12 hours with the accumulated juices.

2 Remove the weight after 24 hours for a lighter texture. Remove the salmon from the marinade, scrape away the herb mixture, and pat dry. The salmon will keep for 5 days, beyond that time it will become a little salty.

3 **Sauce:** Thoroughly combine remaining honey mustard, sour cream, and 1/2 cup fresh dill in a small mixing bowl. Cover and refrigerate until ready to use.

4 Thinly slice the salmon across the grain, on a diagonal to the skin, cutting away from the skin. The skin may be sliced into strips and roasted or sautéed until crisp, to create "salmon cracklings". Serve with mustard dill sauce.

Gravlax is a Scandinavian preparation of raw salmon cured with salt, sugar, herbs, and spices. The marinating action of the salt/sugar cure is likened to the cooking action of lemon or lime juice on fish, with the great advantage of never heating up your already hot summer kitchen. Traditionally served with a sweetened mustard sauce, ice-cold vodka, aquavit, or dry white wine.

2 1/2 lb salmon filet, boned and skin on, halved lengthwise

1 cup fresh dill, coarsely chopped

1/2 cup kosher salt

1/2 cup sugar

1 teaspoon cracked black pepper

1 teaspoon cracked allspice

1/4 cup aquavit liqueur

1 cup honey mustard

1 cup sour cream

1/2 cup fresh dill, chopped

Filet adorned with succulent shrimp for elegant or casual dining.

JESS & JIM'S
STEAK HOUSE

515 E. 135th St., Kansas City, MO
(816)941-9499

The sign outside Jess & Jim's Steak House could very well read "Harry Truman Ate Here." That's because he did. In fact, he called Jess & Jim's steaks the finest in Kansas City. But Truman was just one of many who have touted the qualities of the family-owned and operated restaurant. Awards and laudations line the walls from the likes of USA Today, The Squire, Persona Magazine and Playboy Magazine. Good service, fair prices and a menu featuring not only their excellent steaks but delicious chicken and seafood entrees - it's no wonder Jess & Jim's Steak House is known as one of the top places for steaks in the United States.

Van Noy's Steak and Scampi

PrepTime: 10 minutes
Cooking Time: 10-15 minutes
Servings Per Recipe: 4

1 In a sauté pan, over low heat, combine butter, garlic, lemon juice, white wine, and Tabasco. Add shallots and breadcrumbs to mixture. Blend well. Add shrimp and stir occasionally to coat shrimp. Allow the shrimp to cook until they are plump and firm, approximately 12 minutes.

2 While the shrimp is cooking, wrap each filet with two pieces of bacon. Coat with oil and season to taste. Grill the filets to your liking.

3 Place one cooked filet on each plate. Using a slotted serving spoon, remove the shrimp from the pan and place five shrimp on top of each filet. To complete this meal, serve with a baked potato, pickled beets, and homemade garlic toast.

4 oz butter (one stick)

1 clove garlic, peeled and smashed

1/4 cup lemon juice, fresh squeezed

2 cups white wine

1 teaspoon tabasco sauce

1 cup shallots, chopped

1 cup breadcrumbs

20 large shrimp, peeled and deveined

8 slices of bacon

4 (8-ounce) filet mignon

Olive oil

Salt and pepper (to taste)

Soulfish SEAFOOD GRILL

11723 Roe Ave., Leawood, KS
(913)451-4515

Soulfish Seafood Grill offers the Kansas City dining scene a new and unique style of cuisine - New Southern. Though the emphasis is on seafood, the Soulfish also offers many other excellent selections such as Brown Sugar Maple Cured Pork Chops with Green Apple Chutney, and Pecan Smoked Fried Chicken Breast with Serrano Chili Grits. Other seafood favorites include Peach Barbecue Shrimp, Spiced Red Ahi with Yellow Tomato Salsa, and Tempura Battered Soft Shell Crabs with Chipotle Chili Sauce. A large copper topped salad bar is also featured.

This fantastic Michael Forbes Group restaurant features eclectic Southern style decor and an easy-going casual dining experience. Try it soon.

With Maple butter, green rice, and hush puppies

Pecan Catfish

PrepTime: 20 minutes
Cooking Time: 30 minutes
Servings Per Recipe: 2

1 **Maple Butter:** Combine 8 tablespoons of butter and maple syrup in a small mixing bowl. Blend well. Set aside.

2 **Green Rice:** Puree basil, cilantro, spinach and garlic in a food processor. Boil chicken stock in 1-quart saucepan. Add pureed herbs and rice. Mix well. Bring back to a boil. Simmer 15-20 minutes until rice is tender. Cool slightly. Quickly whisk in egg. Season with salt and pepper. Set aside; keep warm.

3 **Hush Puppies:** Heat a fryer to 350° F. Combine deviled crab mix and cornmeal. Mix well. Scoop into 2 tablespoon-size balls. Fry until golden brown. Place onto paper towel to absorb excess oil.

4 **Catfish:** Combine seasoned flour and pecans in a food processor until somewhat fine. Dredge catfish in mixture. Heat 2 tablespoons butter over medium heat in a large sauté pan. Add breaded catfish. Sauté 3-4 minutes on each side.

5 **Serving:** Place rice and hush puppies on plate. Melt maple butter. Place catfish on plate, then drizzle with butter. Enjoy.

10 tablespoons butter, softened

1/4 cup maple syrup

1/2 bunch fresh basil

1/2 bunch fresh cilantro

1/4 cup fresh spinach, packed

1 tablespoon garlic, minced

1 1/2 cups chicken stock

1 cup basmati rice

1 egg

Salt and pepper (to taste)

1/2 cup deviled crab mix

1/4 cup cornmeal

1 cup flour, seasoned with salt and pepper (to taste)

1 cup pecans, toasted

2 (8-ounce) catfish filets

427 Main , Kansas City, MO (816)421-CLUB

The only thing you won't like about Club 427 is deciding what you like best: the incredible live jazz or the incredibly fine food.

Club 427 continues to be lauded as one of the most happening and most delicious dining destinations on the Kansas City scene. Patrons get an earful of local and national jazz artists and a mouth-watering helping of hand-trimmed steaks, fresh seasoned pasta and catch-of-the-day seafood dishes prepared to order.

By combining live Kansas City-style jazz with a contemporary, exciting atmosphere and critically acclaimed dining, Club 427 has created an entertainment experience reminiscent of New York, LA and Chicago.

Fresh seafood steeped in a rich tomato seafood stock

Calamari Fettuccine De Mare

PrepTime: 15 minutes
Cooking Time: 5 minutes
Servings Per Recipe: 1

1 **Pasta:** Bring 2 quarts water to a boil. Add fettuccine and boil to al dente. Drain. Set aside.

2 Heat olive oil, shallots, garlic, red peppers, and mussels over medium heat in a large sauté pan until shells begin to open. Add tomatoes and fish; sauté until fish begins to change color on the outside. Add stock, then the shrimp. When the seafood is finished cooking add pasta and butter. Heat thoroughly. Season with crushed red peppers and salt and pepper. Enjoy.

Fresh pasta is highly recommended. It has more flavor and cooks much faster than dried pasta. If using dried pasta, you will need to follow the instruction on the package. You may cook the pasta ahead of time (1-2 days) by cooking it in boiling water for 1 minute, stirring constantly. Drain the pasta and "shock" it by dropping it in ice water until it is completely chilled. Drain the water thoroughly and oil the pasta lightly. Wrap tightly until use. You can reheat for 30 seconds in boiling water or in the sauce prior to serving.

5 oz calamari seasoned fettucini (can be purchased at food specialty shop)

1 tablespoon olive oil

1 teaspoon shallots, chopped

1/3 tablespoon garlic, chopped

1 1/2 oz red peppers

3 mussels, shells scrubbed well and debearded removed

1/2 medium tomato, diced

2 oz salmon, tuna, or other seafood

3/4 cup seafood stock (in a pinch, chicken stock can be used)

1 1/2 oz rock shrimp

1 teaspoon butter

Pinch crushed red pepper

Salt and pepper (to taste)

**209 W. 46th Terr., Kansas City, MO
(816)561-0505**

*Delicious Italian dishes with a twist perfectly
describes Figlio's Restaurant & Bar.*

*Executive Chef Scott Allen offers both traditional
Italian entrees as well as a selection of contemporary
interpretations. Specialties include pizzas baked in a
wood-burning oven, handmade fresh pastas and sweet
"dolce" desserts.*

*A strolling accordion player during dinner adds a
touch of real Italy to the night, and on Sundays,
Figlio's celebrates with Brunch Italian-style.*

*A mouth watering shrimp and basil dish
tossed in angel hair pasta and olive oil.*

Capellini with Shrimp

PrepTime: 5 minutes
Cooking Time: 10 minutes
Servings Per Recipe: 2

1 Heat olive oil over medium heat in a large sauté pan. Add garlic, basil, shrimp, tomatoes, salt, and white pepper. Bring to a simmer.

2 Heat the precooked pasta. Add to the pan and mix well with all of the ingredients.

3 Separate pasta on 2 plates. Divide the remaining ingredients on top of the pasta. Garnish each dish with a fresh lemon wedge.

Don't let the oil get too hot to brown the garlic. This dish works best with fresh basil. If you like garlic, add extra. You can substitute scallops, clams, or mussels, for the shrimp.

1/2 cup extra virgin olive oil

1 1/2 tablespoons fresh garlic, chopped

3 tablespoons fresh basil, julienned

3/4 cup bay shrimp

3/4 cup vine ripened tomatoes, chopped

1/4 teaspoon salt

1/8 teaspoon white pepper

1 lb angel hair pasta, cooked

2 lemon wedges (1/6 cut)

J. gilbert's wood-fired steaks

8901 Metcalf, Overland Park, KS
(913)642-8070

Named after the late Joe Gilbert who founded Gilbert/Robinson, J. Gilberts Wood Fired Steaks dining room welcomes each guest with comfortable booths, soft lighting, dark wood, exposed rock walls, and historic Kansas City scenes captured in the many pictures on the J. Gilberts' restaurant walls.

The menu features Black Angus Beef. From mesquite grilled filets to 24-ounce porterhouses, it's a steak lover's dream come true. Other favorites include Barbecued Salmon, Jamaican Chicken and the ever popular Louisiana Skillet-Seared Pepper Filet.

The well-balanced menu and friendly hospitality keep guests returning to J. Gilberts Wood Fired Steaks.

Penne pasta tossed with blackened
chicken and a roasted red pepper sauce

Chicken Penne Pasta

PrepTime: 30 minutes
Cooking Time: 10 minutes
Servings Per Recipe: 2

1 **Roasted Peppers:** Preheat a grill. Place red peppers on grill and char on all sides. Remove and place in a paper bag. Let the peppers stand in a closed bag for 20 minutes. Remove peppers from the bag, peel and seed. Use one pepper for sauce and slice the other for garnish.

2 **Chicken:** Season the chicken breast with blackening spice. Place on grill; cook on both sides until juices run clear. Let chicken cool. Then slice into 1/4-inch slices. Set aside.

3 **Pasta:** Boil pasta in salted water until tender. Cool in cold water. Strain and lightly oil.

4 **Sauce:** Puree one roasted pepper, chicken stock, 2 teaspoons blackening seasoning, and a pinch of salt in blender. Remove and mix with cream. Set aside.

5 **Finishing:** Heat one-quarter cup olive oil over medium-high heat in a large sauté pan. Add garlic; sauté until tender, careful not to burn the garlic. Add snow peas, and leeks; sauté until tender. Add the blackened chicken; sauté 2 more minutes then add the sauce, pasta, one cup cheese, and cilantro. Let sauce reduce by one third. Place in pasta bowls. Garnish with cheese, red pepper and cilantro. Enjoy!

2 red bell peppers

1 lb chicken breast

2 teaspoons blackened seasoning (plus as needed)

1 lb penne pasta

Pinch of salt

1/2 cup chicken stock

3 cups heavy cream

1/4 cup olive oil (plus as needed)

2 tablespoons garlic, chopped

1 cup snow peas, julienned

1 cup leeks, sliced

1 1/4 cups smoked Gouda cheese

1/4 cup fresh cilantro, roughly chopped

Fresh cilantro sprigs (to garnish)

Fiorella's

Now
JACK SMOKE STACK | JACK STACK
BARBECUE | BARBECUE
OF MARTIN CITY | OF OVERLAND PARK
135th & HOLMES | 95th & METCALF

13441 Holmes, Martin City, MO
(816)942-9141

9520 Metcalf Ave., Overland Park, KS
(913)385-7427

*Kansas City is famous for its barbecue and Fiorella's
Jack Stack of Martin City is one of Kansas City's
most famous barbecue spots. In business since 1957,
it's still run by the Fiorella family, serving gourmet
hickory wood cooking prepared in brick ovens.*

*Fiorella's just may have the most extensive barbecue
menu in the country, including seafood items grilled
over hickory wood in addition to their traditional
selections of barbecued meats.*

*Walk into the dining room of Fiorella's Jack Stack of
Martin City and you immediately feel at home. The
atmosphere is warm and cozy, especially next to one
of the wood-burning fireplaces. The Victorian decor
and family memorabilia simply add to the ambience.*

*Come experience the Fiorella family's basic
philosophy of providing consistent culinary quality
and dedication to customer satisfaction.*

Zesty chicken tenders grilled over
hickory wood

Painted Chicken Tenders

PrepTime: 10 minutes
Cooking Time: 10 minutes
Servings Per Recipe: 1

1 Prepare a grill with hickory wood. Heat between 350° and 375° F. Place chicken tenders on a skewer. Rub with Jack Stack Steak Rub. Grill for approximately 3 minutes on each side. Baste with Jack Stack's Mexican barbecue sauce. Grill for another minute. Sprinkle with cheeses and cook until melted. Serve with a side of barbecue sauce.

10 (1 oz) chicken tenders

1/2 cup Jack Stack's Steak Rub

1/4 cup Jack Stack's Mexican barbecue sauce (or other favorite BBQ sauce)

1 1/2 oz Monterey jack cheese, grated

1 1/2 oz cheddar cheese, grated

KC Masterpiece
Barbecue & Grill

10985 Metcalf, Overland Park, KS
(913)345-8646

4747 Wyandotte, Kansas City, MO
(816) 531-3332

KC Masterpiece specializes in authentic, closed-pit barbecuing, a cooking method resulting in flavors and textures that can't be duplicated by any other method.

In the grand tradition of the barbecue, KC's atmosphere is casual yet classy at the same time. They boast a diverse menu including barbecued burnt ends, baby back ribs, brisket, chicken, steaks, burgers and salads.

KC Masterpiece's Hickory Platter is an excellent sampler of several hickory-smoked favorites. Or try the Onion Straws and Doc's Dip, popular pre-dinner warm ups.

For the best in barbecue any time, KC Masterpiece is the place.

Juicy, seasoned half chicken with KC Masterpiece barbecue sauce

Smoked Chicken

PrepTime: 15 minutes
Cooking Time: 120 minutes
Servings Per Recipe: 2

1 **Dry Rub:** Thoroughly combine brown sugar, black pepper, paprika, chile powder, salt and garlic powder in a mixing bowl. Set aside.

2 Fold wing back and break leg of chicken. Pull off tail and excess fat. Coat entire chicken heavily with dry rub mix. Marinate the chicken in the dry rub for 4-24 hours. (The flavor from the dry rub will be more pronounced as the marinating time increases.)

3 **Cooking Options:** The chicken may be cooked using a smoker or a grill.

4 **Smoker Cooking:** Prepare smoker with enough coals to last approximately 2-3 hours. Place water-soaked wood chunks (KC Masterpiece uses hickory wood) on top of coals. The temperature should register 200-225° F at meat level. Place the chicken bone-side down and meat-side up; smoke for approximately 2-3 hours. Baste with KC Masterpiece barbecue sauce approximately 30 minutes before removing from the smoker. Chicken will be done when the meat has pulled away from the bone.

5 **Grilling:** Start charcoals and let them burn down to white on the outside. Leave the charcoal mounded up on one side of the grill. Place water-soaked hickory chunks on the charcoal. The temperature should register 200-225° F at meat level. Place the chicken bone-side down and meat-side up. Close the lid on the grill leaving any vents slightly open. Smoke for approximately 2-3 hours. Baste with KC Masterpiece barbecue sauce approximately 30 minutes before removing from the smoker. Chicken will be done when the meat has pulled away from the bone.

1/2 cup brown sugar

1/2 cup black pepper, coarsely ground

1/2 cup paprika

1/4 cup chile powder

1/4 cup salt

2 tablespoons garlic powder

1 whole chicken, cut in half

KC Masterpiece barbecue sauce (as needed)

THE MARINA GROG AND GALLEY

Gate 1 at Waters Edge, Lake Lotawana, MO
(816)578-5511

There's only one place in all of Kansas City where you can dine on grilled ostrich and Portabella mushrooms in uniquely elegant surroundings and with a lovely view of the lake. Let's be frank, there's only one place like this in all of Missouri and that's the Marina Grog & Galley. Executive chef Amy Presson can't take credit for the lake, but she can and does take credit for the excellent variety of appetizers and entrees including the grilled ostrich and equally ambitious seafood, beef, poultry and pasta dishes. And you won't want to pass up the excellent selection of in-house smoked items. An excitingly different menu and a beautiful setting, it's no wonder the Marina Grog and Galley is one of the Midwest's premier dining destinations.

Scallops baked with garlic butter and Gruyère cheese

Baked Scallops

PrepTime: 45 minutes
Cooking Time: 15-20 minutes
Servings Per Recipe: 1

1 **Garlic Butter:** Blend butter, garlic, lemon juice, Worcestershire, black pepper, and parsley thoroughly together in a bowl. Cover and chill.

2 **Scallops:** Preheat oven to 350° F. Place scallops on the bottom of a small casserole dish and sprinkle with wine. Add garlic butter pieces and sprinkle with cheese. Top with breadcrumbs. Bake for 15-20 minutes or until scallops are no longer opaque.

1/2 lb butter, softened

1 teaspoon garlic, minced

1 teaspoon fresh lemon juice

1/2 teaspoon Worcestershire sauce

1/4 teaspoon black pepper, coarse grind

1/4 teaspoon parsley, chopped

10-12 sea scallops

2 tablespoons white wine

1 1/2 tablespoons garlic butter, chilled and cut into 4 pieces

1/3 cup Gruyère cheese, grated

1/3 cup fresh breadcrumbs

LODGE
Charlie's

7953 State Line, Kansas City, MO
(816)333-6363

Experience the warm and inviting ambience of Charlie's Lodge with a nice relaxing lunch or dinner by the fire.

Charlie's Lodge serves delicious steaks, seafood, salads and pasta dishes for all to enjoy.

Owner Charles Penner offers a unique and individual touch to make Charlie's Lodge a relaxing and fabulous restaurant.

Sautéed shrimp in a white wine cream sauce with seafood ravioli

Seafood Ravioli

PrepTime: 4 minutes
Cooking Time: 4 minutes
Servings Per Recipe: 1

1 Heat olive oil over medium heat in a large sauté pan. Add shrimp, then sauté until shrimp are pink in color. Add the tomatoes, garlic, and basil. Sauté until tomatoes have warmed a bit. Add heavy cream and white wine to the pan. Then add the ravioli. Sauté until the ravioli have warmed through. Add Parmesan to thicken the sauce and season with salt and pepper, to taste. Sauté until thickened a touch and serve hot.

The seafood ravioli the restaurant uses are filled with crab, lobster, garlic, onion, celery, and ricotta cheese.

1 teaspoon olive oil

6 large (16-20 per pound) shrimp, peeled and deveined

1/2 cup tomatoes, diced

1 teaspoon garlic, peeled and chopped

1 teaspoon basil, chopped

1 cup heavy cream

1/2 cup white wine

5 seafood ravioli (available at specialty markets)

1/2 cup Parmesan cheese, grated

Salt and pepper (to taste)

Cascone's

**3733 N. Oak Trfwy., Kansas City, MO
(816)454-7977**

One of Kansas City's most well-known Italian restaurants, Cascone's has been serving Kansas Citians and their visitors for over 60 years. Family members attribute their business success to close attention to detail in everything that they do.

Cascone's culinary specialties range from such traditional Italian favorites as Lasagna, Veal Parmigiana and Chicken Spedini to signature dishes like Chicken Limonata Elaina, Tortellom Savina Marie and Stuffed Artichokes.

From the photographs of Italian families on the walls to the sounds of Sinatra in the air, Cascone's is casual and comfortable. They strive to make their guests feel welcome, as though they're sitting at "Mama's" table in their best friend's house, eating the best food they have ever had.

Cascone's also offers a wide range of "non-Italian" fare such as steaks, chops and fresh seafood daily.

A wonderful beginning with truly unique flavors of Italy

Stuffed Artichoke Hearts

PrepTime: 20 minutes
Cooking Time: 45 minutes
Servings Per Recipe: 4

1 Remove the stems from the artichokes so they will stand up. Lay the artichokes on sides and cut about 1-inch off the top with a sharp knife. Trim 1/4-inch off tops of all leaf points with scissors. Rub artichokes with lemon juice to prevent discoloration. Place the artichokes upside down in a large enamel kettle with 3 cups of water; bring to a boil, cover and cook for about 10 minutes. Drain and cool. Pull out the inner core of the thistle-like leaves to expose the choke, also known as the "heart" and continue to clean thoroughly, leaving the heart clean.

2 Heat olive oil over medium heat in a large sauté pan; add garlic and sauté until soft. Remove from heat and mix in breadcrumbs, grated cheese, parsley, salt and pepper. Mix together loosely.

3 Preheat oven to 350° F. Open outer leaves of the artichoke and fill loosely with the breadcrumb mixture, stuffing centers of the artichoke with light amounts of the mixture and the mushrooms. Place artichokes in a baking pan. Add the chicken broth and cover tightly with foil. Bake for about 45 minutes; remove the foil during the last 15 minutes, allowing to lightly brown. Serve hot with drizzled butter and lemon wedges.

4 large artichokes, stemmed

1/2 cup lemon juice

3 cups water

1/2 cup olive oil

1 clove garlic, peeled and minced

2 cups seasoned breadcrumbs

1/2 cup Italian cheese, grated

2 tablespoons minced parsley

Salt and pepper (to taste)

1/2 cup sliced mushrooms

1 cup chicken broth

1/2 cup butter, melted (hot)

Lemon wedges (to garnish)

A zesty Southwestern soup

4843 Johnson Dr., Shawnee, KS (913)362-3333

Santa Fe, New Mexico may have provided the inspiration for the Coyote Grill, but it's the unique touches Paul Khoury and Bill Crooks added that make Midwesterners feel right at home in this adobe-style restaurant.

It is appetizers like the Texas Goat Cheese Tamale and the Barbecue Shrimp Enchilada that has earned Coyote Grill a place on the Zagat Kansas City Restaurant Survey lists for Most Popular and Top Late Night restaurants.

A bustling bistro with a tantalizing Southwestern menu, it is fair to say the Coyote Grill is a howling success.

Tortilla Soup

PrepTime: 30 minutes
Cooking Time: 20 minutes
Servings Per Recipe: 6

1 Heat a deep fryer to 350° F. Add tortillas and fry until golden brown. Place tortillas on paper towels to absorb excess oil. Season with salt and pepper. Reserve half for garnish, use the rest for the soup.

2 Heat bacon grease over medium heat in a 3-quart sauce pot. Add onions, garlic, peppers and thyme; sauté until onions are tender. Add chicken stock, tomatoes, corn tortillas, chili powder and cumin; mix well. Continue to cook until tortillas are soft. Strain through a food mill. Season with salt and pepper. (If soup is too thick, add chicken stock to thin.)

3 Ladle into bowls and garnish with Monterey Jack and cheddar cheeses, fresh avocado and fried corn tortilla strips.

8 oz corn tortillas, cut into strips

Oil (for frying)

Salt and pepper (to taste)

1/4 cup bacon grease

1 white onion, peeled and diced

1 oz garlic, peeled and minced

2 Anaheim peppers, diced

1/2 jalapeño pepper, diced

2 red bell peppers, diced

1/2 tablespoon thyme

1/2 gallon chicken stock

1/4 cup tomatoes, diced

1/4 cup tomatoes, crushed

1 1/2 cups chili powder

1/2 cup cumin

1 cup Monterey Jack cheese, shredded (to garnish)

1 cup cheddar cheese, shredded (to garnish)

1 avocado, diced (to garnish)

CLASSIC BAR & CAFE
BRASSERIE

Westin Crown Center, Kansas City, MO
(816)371-4472

Canopies and old-fashioned light posts on the boulevard welcome guests to the Brasserie Cafe at the Westin Crown Center.

This European-style bistro offers a casual dining experience with a menu that features a combination of traditional and new American cuisine.

After dinner, enjoy cocktails in the Brasserie Lounge. The Brasserie also offers a scrumptious daily buffet for breakfast, lunch and dinner.

Roasted chicken with Yukon Gold mashed potatoes

Rosemary Roasted Chicken

PrepTime: 10 minutes
Cooking Time: 40 minutes
Servings Per Recipe: 4

1 **Chicken:** Preheat oven to 350° F. Wash chickens, dry and truss. Combine garlic, rosemary, and olive oil in a small bowl. Rub chicken thoroughly with olive oil mixture. Season with salt and pepper. Place into a roasting pan. Cook for 35-40 minutes, or until done.

2 **Mashed Potatoes:** Place potatoes in a medium pot. Cover with cold water. Bring to a simmer. Simmer until tender. Strain potatoes and let cool 1 1/2 minutes in collander. Place into a mixing bowl. Mash with mixer or masher until smooth. Fold in cream and butter. Season with salt and pepper, to taste.

3 **Serving:** Remove chicken meat from bones. Place one serving of mash potatoes in the center of each serving plate. Neatly arrange chicken around potatoes. Enjoy.

2 whole chickens

2 teaspoons garlic, chopped

1 tablespoon fresh rosemary, chopped

1/4 olive oil

2 teaspoons sea salt (to taste)

2 teaspoons fresh ground black pepper (to taste)

1 lb Yukon Gold potatoes, peeled

1/2 cup heavy cream

2 tablespoons unsalted butter

RISTORANTE

10819 E. 40 Hwy., Independence, MO
(816)353-1241

Long known as Kansas City's premier Italian restaurant, this family-owned and operated establishment has been an important part of the city for over 30 years.

V's Italiano Ristorante's formula for pleasing its guests is simply combining uncompromised service in a beautiful, relaxed environment. The menu features a wide variety of authentic Italian specialties as well as steaks, poultry and seafood - all at moderate prices.

If you're searching for a place for a romantic dinner for two, come see why V's Italiano is known around town as "a nice place to fall in love". V's also is home to the "Best Sunday Brunch in Town" and an award-winning wine list. V's Italiano is the area's "must see" Italian restaurant.

Broiled lightly breaded skewered shrimp with Italian mogue

Shrimp Spiedini

PrepTime: 15 minutes
Cooking Time: 10 minutes
Servings Per Recipe: 2

1 **Mogue:** Combine olive oil, tomato, diced garlic, and basil in a small sauce pan. Warm over medium heat. When the mixture is hot, remove from heat and let stand.

2 **Shrimp:** Thoroughly combine breadcrumbs, Romano cheese, 1 teaspoon garlic powder, white pepper, seasoned salt, and parsley flakes in a bowl. Set aside.

3 Thoroughly combine melted butter, diced garlic and 1 teaspoon garlic powder in a bowl. Set aside.

4 Thread 6 shrimp, through head and tail, onto each skewer. Repeat with remaining shrimp. Brush with garlic butter, then dredge in the breadcrumbs. Broil until tender and golden brown.

5 **Fettuccine Alfredo:** Heat cream over medium heat in a medium sauté pan. Add Romano cheese and stir until cheese has melted. Add fettuccine and toss until well coated.

6 **Serving:** Place broiled shrimp on a bed of Fettuccine Alfredo. Top with warm mogue. Garnish with parsley and lemon.

For the Mogue:

1/4 cup olive oil

1 medium tomato, diced

4 whole cloves garlic, peeled and diced

4 fresh basil leaves, diced

For the Shrimp:

1 1/2 cups Italian breadcrumbs

1/4 cup Romano cheese, grated

2 teaspoons garlic powder (divided)

1 teaspoon white pepper

1 teaspoon seasoned salt

1 tablespoon parsley flakes

4 oz butter, melted

4 cloves garlic, peeled and diced

12 jumbo shrimp, peeled and deveined

2 wooden skewers

For the Fettuccine Alfredo:

6 oz fettuccine pasta, cooked

1 cup heavy cream

3/4 cup Romano cheese, grated

For the Garnish:

2 tablespoons fresh parsley, chopped

2 lemon wedges

O'DOWD'S LITTLE DUBLIN
Irish Ale House and Pub

4742 Pennsylvania, Kansas City, MO
(816)561-2700

Take a trip to Ireland via O'Dowd's Little Dublin on the Country Club Plaza. Named for the legendary Mr. O'Dowd, a sportsman, raconteur and imbiber who held court every night at his Victorian pub in turn-of-the century Dublin, Kansas City's O'Dowd's captures the same spirit of fun and good times exemplified by "The Old Man" himself.

O'Dowd's Little Dublin not only offers the finest Irish stout, ale and whiskey, but boasts a wonderful array of hearty Irish dishes, like the traditional "Irish Boxty" stew, steaks, Dublin coddle and sandwiches. Executive Chef Chris Rixner spent time in Ireland working with Irish chefs to create his menu and has earned a 3 out of 4 stars rating from the Kansas City Star and 3 stars in Mobile Travel Guide.

Live music on Tuesday, Wednesday, Saturday & Sunday featuring Bob Reeder and Eddie Decantunt, the only thing missing from O'Dowd's Little Dublin is the old man himself.

Grilled chicken breast with fried vegetables with Murphy's Amber Glaze

Amber Chicken Brushetts

PrepTime: 10 minutes
Cooking Time: 10 minutes
Servings Per Recipe: 2

1 **Amber glaze:** Thoroughly combine ketchup, mustard, English mustard, molasses, orange juice, brown sugar, garlic powder, 1/2 teaspoon black pepper, 1/4 teaspoon salt, ale, Worcestershire, and Tabasco in a nonreactive bowl. Set aside.

2 **Chicken:** Remove any fat and cartilage from the chicken. Slice chicken on a bias angle into 12 pieces. Season chicken with salt and pepper, to taste. Grill or roast chicken until tender and juicy. Let cool. Thread each piece of chicken on a skewer. Set aside.

3 **Fried vegetables:** Heat oil to 350° F in a deep fryer or large pot. Fry the julienned potatoes until golden brown. Place on paper towelling to drain excess oil. Season with salt and pepper, to taste. Repeat with sweet potato, followed by the leek. Set aside.

4 **Finishing:** Preheat oven to 300° F. Slice baked potato in half. Place on baking sheet along with chicken skewers. Place in oven for 5 minutes, or until thoroughly heated.

5 **Assemble:** Place each half of potato on a plate with the ends of six skewers inserted into potato. Take a small handful of sweet potato straws and place inside skewers, lightly stacking upward, follow with white potato straws, then leeks. Drizzle each plate entirely with glaze. Garnish plate rim with chopped parsley.

1/2 cup ketchup

1/4 cup mustard

1/4 cup English mustard

1/4 cup molasses

1/4 cup orange juice

1/4 cup brown sugar

1/4 teaspoon garlic powder

1/2 teaspoon black pepper (plus to taste)

1/4 teaspoon salt (plus to taste)

1/3 cup Murphy's Amber Ale (or other amber ale)

Dash of Worcestershire sauce

Dash of Tabasco sauce

2 (6-ounce) chicken breasts

1 potato, julienned

1 sweet potato, julienned

1 leek, green part only, julienned

2 cups oil (for deep frying)

1 baked potato

2 tablespoons parsley, chopped (to garnish)

Timberline Steakhouse & Grill's famous baby back ribs

TIMBERLINE STEAKHOUSE & GRILL

ALTITUDE iS EVERYThING!™

920 N.E. Columbus St., Lee's Summit, MO
(816)554-3323

2243 N. Tyler, Wichita, KS
(316)773-3111

At the Timberline Steakhouse the idea is to chill out. In fact, they don't even mind if you drop a few peanut shells on the floor. You'll find the Timberline a place where you can kick back and relax with plenty of good food to go around.

In keeping with the restaurant's mountain theme, menu items are appropriately named High Sierra Onion Blossom, Himalayan Porterhouse, Alpine Pasta and Smoke Shack Avalanche BBQ Sampler.

You could say the Timberline Steakhouse takes casual dining to new heights because at Timberline, ALTITUDE IS EVERYTHING!

Baby Back Ribs

PrepTime: 20 minutes
Cooking Time: 180 minutes
Servings Per Recipe: 4-6

1 **Rib Rub:** Thoroughly combine seasoned salt, 1 tablespoon black pepper, sugar, garlic powder, and garlic salt in a bowl.

2 **Rib Preparation:** Insert a stiff knife under the skin on the backside of the first (smallest) bone. Work the skin loose. Using a towel to help grasp the skin, peel off as much of the skin as possible. Lightly coat the ribs with rib rub. Cover and refrigerate until the ribs are ready to be seared off.

3 **Cooking of ribs:** Preheat oven to 325° F. Toss the onions with vegetable oil and 1/2 teaspoon black pepper. Place on a baking sheet in the bottom of the oven. Roast 30 minutes or until onions are golden brown. While onions are roasting, sear the ribs on an outdoor grill. Starting with the concave side down, sear the ribs until marked and well-colored. Turn the ribs and brush with barbecue sauce. Continue searing until the underside is browned. Coat other side with barbecue sauce. Remove from the grill and arrange on a baking sheet.

4 When the onions are golden brown, combine the liquid smoke and water. Pour into the baking sheet with the onions. Place the pan of ribs into the oven on the rack above the onions. Roast for 3 hours. Ribs should be brushed with barbecue sauce and serve.

These ribs can be done ahead of time and reheated on your grill or in your oven.

5 oz seasoned salt

1 tablespoon + 1/2 teaspoon coarse ground black pepper

2 tablespoons white sugar

1 tablespoon garlic powder

1 tablespoon garlic salt

4 racks (1 3/4-2 lb) pork baby back ribs

1 medium onion, skin on, quartered

1 tablespoon vegetable oil

1 quart Timberline Steakhouse & Grill BBQ sauce (or your favorite)

2 tablespoons liquid smoke

1 cup water

Italian Gardens

1110 Baltimore, Kansas City, MO
(816)221-9311

Italian Gardens has been a downtown Kansas City tradition for nearly a hundred years.

Long appreciated for its dedication to bringing patrons the best in traditional Italian cuisine, the Italian Gardens continues to be the destination of choice for the discriminating diner.

The menu offers expertly executed, all-time favorite Italian dishes and an accompanying wine list features an excellent selection of wines. A hallmark on the Kansas City dining scene, Italian Gardens consistently pleases.

A warm and inviting lasagna for everyone

Lasagna

PrepTime: 30 minutes
Cooking Time: 20 minutes
Servings Per Recipe: 9

1 Preheat oven to 350° F. Cook lasagna noodles in boiling salted
water until al dente, about 20 minutes. Drain. Lay lasagna in a single
layer across the bottom of a 9 x 15-inch pan that is 2-3 inches deep.
Fill with half the mozzarella cheese, then half the ricotta cheese. Place
3 layers of noodles on top (forming the middle layer). Then place
another layer of mozzarella cheese, followed by remaining ricotta
cheese. Place a single layer of noodles on top. Cover with tomato
sauce (the restaurant uses their famous Italian Gardens sauce). Place
in oven. Cook briefly until the cheese has melted, approximately 20
minutes. Cut into 3-inch or 4-inch squares. Sprinkle with grated
cheese and serve. Enjoy.

Your favorite homemade or prepared pasta or marinara sauce may be
used.

1 lb lasagna noodles

1/2 lb mozzarella cheese, thinly sliced

3/4 lb ricotta cheese

1 cup tomato sauce

2 cups Parmigiano cheese, grated

of New Orleans

11920 Metcalf Ave., Overland Park, KS
(913)663-5290

Enjoy a little Mardi Gras in Kansas City at Copeland's, featuring Cajun-American cuisine with such classics as Blackened Shrimp, Crawfish Etouffee, and Shrimp and Redfish Creole. Copeland's also offers a more hearty fare with prime rib and delicious steaks. And, the Fried Seafood Platter is a sight to behold with mounds of seafood, corn fritters and onion rings.

Top the meal off with one of Copeland's homemade desserts, Sweet Potato Pecan Bread Pudding, Chocolate Lover's Dream, or The Chocolate Glace, Homemade Cheesecake or the traditional New Orleans classic Bananas Foster, just to name a few.

Blackened pork tenders with a creamy mushroom sauce over angel hair pasta

Blackened Pork La Boucherie

PrepTime: 30 minutes
Cooking Time: 25 minutes
Servings Per Recipe: 4

1 Sprinkle pork medallions with blackening seasoning and set aside.

2 Heat olive oil over medium-high heat in a sauce pan, then add the onions, peppers, and garlic. Sauté until the onions have become translucent, then add the mushrooms and other spices. Simmer until the mushrooms become tender. Deglaze the pan with the Burgundy wine, then add the beef stock and bring to a boil. Lower heat to a simmer, and add the heavy cream. Reduce until the sauce thickens.

3 Boil pasta in salted water until al dente. Drain; set aside.

4 Heat a cast iron skillet until very hot, then dip seasoned pork in clarified butter, and blacken in skillet to desired temperature.

5 Center the pasta in the 12:00 position of the plate, ladle the sauce onto the plate, and fan the cooked pork over the sauce.

2 pork tenders, peeled and cut into 1/2-inch thick medallions

3 tablespoons blackening seasoning

4 tablespoons olive oil

1/4 cup onion, diced

1/4 cup green peppers, diced

1/4 cup red peppers, diced

1 tablespoon garlic, minced

2 cups mushrooms, sliced

1 teaspoon white pepper

2 teaspoons salt

1/2 teaspoon black ground pepper

2 oz Burgundy wine

2 cups beef stock

2 cups heavy cream

8 oz angel hair pasta

3 oz clarified butter

Johnny Cascone's

6863 W. 91st St., Overland Park, KS
(913)381-6837

Johnny Cascone's Italian Restaurant features a blend of Southern and Northern Italian cuisine, offering many distinct menu items ranging from the traditional red and white sauces to more contemporary dishes using fresh seafood and tender veal, beef and chicken. Known for its Old World style and charm, Johnny Cascone's has become a favorite Italian eatery for those living in South Kansas City.

From the moment you enter, you feel at home as you're greeted by a member of the Cascone family. You'll see the pictures of the local Italian families and celebrities on the walls as you listen to the music of Tony Bennett and Frank Sinatra. It's all what makes Johnny Cascone's famous.

This family recipe is simple and is served often as a featured house special

Chicken Marsala

PrepTime: 10-15 minutes
Cooking Time: 10-12 minutes
Servings Per Recipe: 4

1 Put the chicken breast between 2 pieces of wax paper and pound thin. Coat each piece with flour.

2 Heat olive oil over high heat in a large skillet until it sizzles, add the garlic and stir quickly for about 30-45 seconds. Add chicken and brown on both sides.

3 Reduce the heat. Add sliced mushrooms, peppers, and onions. Sauté briefly. Add the beef bouillon and Marsala wine and deglaze the skillet. Add salt and pepper, to taste. Put on low heat for approximately 7-10 minutes. Serve on a bed of freshly cooked spaghetti tossed with butter. Garnish with fresh chopped parsley.

4 (4 to 6-ounce) chicken breasts, skinned and boned

6 tablespoons flour, seasoned with pepper

1/4 cup olive oil

2 cloves crushed garlic, finely chopped

1/2 lb fresh mushrooms, sliced

1/4 lb green peppers, julienned

1/2 lb onions, julienned

1 cup beef bouillon

1 cup sweet Marsala wine

Salt and pepper (to taste)

1 lb cooked spaghetti

2 tablespoons butter

Chopped fresh parsley

GUADALAJARA
CAFÉ
FINEST MEXICAN CUISINE

1144 West 103 St, Kansas City, MO
(816)941-4471

According to the Guadalajara Cafe, they're not just another Mexican Restaurant, they're "the only one." It's where you can enjoy fantastic authentic Mexican cuisine in an elegant friendly atmosphere.

Guadalajara Cafe is in a class of its own. All of their recipes have been handed down by expert chefs, and are meticulously prepared to produce the freshest full bodied flavor possible.

The food, service and elegant atmosphere have made the Guadalajara Cafe a Kansas City favorite for many years.

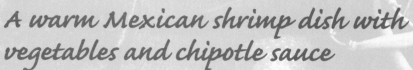

A warm Mexican shrimp dish with vegetables and chipotle sauce

Camarones Al Chipotle

PrepTime: 30 minutes
Cooking Time: 25 minutes
Servings Per Recipe: 4

1 **Chipotle sauce:** Place chipotle peppers, peeled tomatoes, minced garlic, bay leaves, 1 tablespoon olive oil, red onion, and water into a shaker. Shake to mix up. Pour into a 1-quart sauce pan. Bring to a boil over medium heat. Strain off chipotle water for use in preparing shrimp. Puree remaining ingredients in a blender to create a thick sauce.

2 **Shrimp:** Combine shrimp, cream, 1 tablespoon olive oil, 1 teaspoon garlic, 4 tablespoons butter, and 3 1/2 tablespoons of strained chipotle water in a large skillet. Cook over medium heat for 5-6 minutes. Remove shrimp. Set aside; keep warm.

3 **Vegetables:** Combine the vegetables, liquid from shrimp, 1 teaspoon olive oil, 1/2 teaspoon salt, and 1 1/2 tablespoons butter in a large skillet. Cook over medium heat for 3-4 minutes.

4 **Serving:** Combine the chipotle sauce, shrimp and vegetables together. Serve over a bed of Spanish rice. Garnish with chopped tomatoes and chives. Enjoy!

4-6 dried chipotle peppers

2 medium tomatoes, peeled

2 (1/4-inch squares) garlic, minced

4 bay leaves

2 1/2 tablespoons olive oil

1/2 slice red onion

2 cups water

1 lb (27 pieces) large shrimp, peeled, tail on and deveined

4 1/2 tablespoons heavy cream

1 teaspoon garlic, chopped

5 1/2 tablespoons butter

1/3 lb cauliflower florettes

1/3 lb carrots, julienned

1/3 lb broccoli florettes

4 cups Spanish rice, cooked

1 bunch chives, chopped (to garnish)

1 tomato, diced

Paradise Grill

5225 N.W. 64th St., Kansas City, MO
(816)587-9888

The Paradise Grill restaurant teams some of America's favorite foods with new ideas of its own.

There is the house-cured Portabella chop with a portabella mushroom glaze, spinach scalloped potatoes and grilled sweet corn, a delicate balancing act of southwest and northern cuisines. Another favorite is the Shrimp Paradise, ancho chili marinated Gulf shrimp, charbroiled with a jalapeño-cilantro sauce and rice. It is their signature appetizer inspired by Southwestern and Mexican culinary delights.

There is also Chicky-Chicky, marinated oven-roasted breast of chicken with spinach scalloped potatoes, grilled asparagus and a balsamic thyme butter sauce.

Exciting dishes like these along with a center atrium and eye-popping color scheme that have established Paradise Grill as a Kansas City favorite.

Black pepper crusted KC strip with a saké hoisin glaze and Southwestern vegetable glaze

East Meats West

PrepTime: 30 minutes
Cooking Time: 20 minutes
Servings Per Recipe: 6

1 **Hoisin Saké Glaze:** Thoroughly combine hoisin, 1/2 cup sugar, soy sauce, Burgundy, veal stock, and saké in a 3-quart sauce pot. Reduce over medium heat by one-half. Season with salt and pepper. Set aside.

2 **Coulis:** Puree red peppers, onion, 2 cucumbers, chicken stock, garlic, and 1 teaspoon sugar in a blender. Season with salt and pepper; set aside.

3 **Egg Rolls:** Thoroughly combine the julienned cabbage, carrots, cucumbers, chives, cilantro, red chile flakes, and cumin in a large nonreactive bowl. Season with salt and pepper. Lay egg roll wrapper on a flat surface. Place 1/4 cup of mixture on wrapper. Roll according to egg roll wrapper package directions. Seal closed with a dash of water. Heat a deep fryer to 350° F. Fry egg rolls until golden brown. Place on paper towel, allowing excess oil to absorb.

4 **Steaks:** Cover steaks with crushed black pepper on both sides. Heat a grill or broiler. Cook to desired doneness.

5 **Serving:** Cut egg rolls one-third of the way down on a bias. Ladle a small amount of coulis on one-half of the plate. Place the egg rolls in an upright position onto coulis. Place steak next to coulis. Drizzle glaze over the steak and all around the steak. Garnish the plates with a sprinkling of crushed black pepper.

1/2 cup hoisin sauce

1/2 cup + 1 teaspoon sugar

1/2 cup soy sauce

1 cup Burgundy wine

1 1/2 quarts veal stock or good quality chicken stock

2 cups saké

Salt and pepper (to taste)

7 roasted red peppers, charred portions removed

1/2 onion, grilled

2 cucumbers, peeled

1 cup chicken stock

1 teaspoon garlic, minced

1/2 head green cabbage, julienned

1/4 head red cabbage, julienned

2 carrots, julienned

2 cucumbers, peeled, seeded and julienned

1/2 cup chives, cut into 2-inch pieces

1/2 bunch cilantro, chopped

Dash of red chile flakes

Dash of cumin

12 egg roll wrappers

Oil for deep frying

6 (12-ounce) Kansas City strip steaks

1 cup crushed black pepper

Halibut baked in paper with Pomme Duchesse

Teller's

746 Massachusetts, Lawrence, KS
(785)843-4111

Teller's is situated in the historic Merchants National Bank building in downtown Lawrence, thus the name, Teller's.

The high ceilings, unique lighting and warm colors create an atmosphere perfect for unwinding and relaxing. Much of the bank's original architecture has been preserved including the vault, which has been transformed into restrooms. Art by artist Stan Herd, and University of Kansas metallurgist John Havener grace Teller's walls.

Teller's Chef John Beasley was classically schooled at the California Culinary Academy. His culinary style mixes modern Californian cuisine with Old World Mediterranean cooking, a style, you could say, that has generated a lot of interest for Teller's.

Great architecture, great ambiance, great art and great food and wine, Teller's is one restaurant you can bank on.

Halibut en Papillote

PrepTime: 45 minutes
Cooking Time: 60 minutes
Servings Per Recipe: 4

1 Preheat oven to 400° F. Pierce potatoes with a fork. Place in oven and bake until soft, approximately 30-45 minutes.

2 **Fish:** Cut parchment paper into heart shapes, by folding the paper in half, then cutting the outer sides in half of a heart shape. On one side of each piece of parchment paper, place one halibut filet, 1 tablespoon butter, 1 scallion, 2 lemon slices, 2 tablespoons Chardonnay, and season with salt and pepper. Fold over parchment and crimp the edges. Set aside.

3 **Pomme Duchesse:** Remove potatoes from oven. Cut tops off and remove meat of potatoes into a bowl. Mash potatoes with egg yolks, 8 tablespoons butter, cream, nutmeg, and salt and pepper, to taste. Whip together until creamy. Adjust seasoning with salt and pepper, if necessary. Set aside; keep warm.

4 **Finishing:** Place fish on baking sheet. Place in oven. Bake for 8 minutes or until thoroughly cooked. Serve with Pomme Duchesse and steamed vegetables. Enjoy.

4 baking potatoes

4 pieces (12 x 12-inch squares) parchment paper

4 (7-ounce) halibut filets, boned and skinned

12 tablespoons butter

4 scallions, tops and tips removed

1 lemon, cut into 8 slices

8 tablespoons Chardonnay

Salt and pepper (to taste)

4 egg yolks

1/4 cup heavy cream

1 teaspoon nutmeg

Sautéed chicken breast with mushrooms and peppers in a Marsala wine sauce

702 S.E. Blue Pkwy., Lee's Summit, MO
(816)246-1884

Mama Angie's is a one-of-a-kind family-owned and operated family restaurant.

With magicians entertaining on the weekends, a banquet facility painted to resemble a wine cellar, black and white family photos lining the walls and a fireplace that can be seen from any seat in the restaurant, Mama Angie's is a wonderful place to bring the entire family.

Patrons appreciate the reasonable prices and large portions. The food is so good and the atmosphere so much fun, people love coming back.

Chicken Marsala

PrepTime: 10 minutes
Cooking Time: 10 minutes
Servings Per Recipe: 1

1 Lightly pound chicken breast. Season with salt and pepper, then lightly flour. Heat canola oil and butter over medium-high heat in a skillet. Add chicken and brown on each side, approximately 2 1/2 minutes each side. Set aside.

2 Heat olive oil and garlic over medium heat in a medium sauté pan. When hot, add mushrooms, peppers, and onions. Sauté approximately 2 minutes. Add Marsala, then chicken breasts. Simmer for 2 minutes. Place onto a plate and serve with your favorite side dishes.

1 (8-ounce) chicken breast

Salt and pepper (to taste)

Flour (as needed)

1/4 cup canola oil

1/4 cup butter

1 tablespoon virgin olive oil

1/4 teaspoon garlic, minced

2 tablespoons mushrooms

1/4 cup green bell peppers, sliced

1/4 cup red bell peppers, sliced

2 tablespoons onions, sliced

2 tablespoons Marsala wine

Marinated chicken over a cream cheese sauce and pasta

12225 Strangline, Olathe, KS
(913)768-8737

8401 N. Boardwalk Ave., Kansas City, MO
(816)746-9980

Twenty-two years ago, three aspiring restaurateurs came to the Lake of the Ozarks from southwest Arizona with nothing but a dream to open a restaurant and a bunch of old recipes - some as old as three generations - from friends and family.

Such was the birth of one of the best and most successful Mexican restaurants in the area. Appropriately named "Tres Hombres" after its three founders, there are now five Tres Hombres restaurants.

Serving excellent authentic Mexican food in a relaxed friendly atmosphere, be it from ever so humble beginnings, there's no place like Tres Hombres.

Tequila Lime Chicken

PrepTime: 24 minutes
Cooking Time: 25 minutes
Servings Per Recipe: 4-6

1 **Marinade:** Blend canola oil, garlic, onion, lime juice, tequila, cumin, black pepper, cilantro, and 2 teaspoons cayenne pepper together in a nonreactive dish. Add chicken. Cover. Refrigerate 24 hours.

2 **Sauce:** Melt butter over medium heat in a 2-quart saucepan. Whisk in flour, stirring constantly. Add half and half, continuing to stir constantly. Whisk in cream cheese, 1/3 teaspoon cayenne pepper, white pepper, chicken base, and salt. Whisk well until cream cheese melts. Remove from heat; set aside.

3 **Pasta:** Bring 2 quarts water with salt, to taste, to a boil. Add pasta and cook to al dente. Drain well.

4 **Chicken:** Remove chicken from marinade. Grill on both sides until tender, juicy, and thoroughly cooked.

5 **Serving:** Place pasta onto plates. Ladle sauce over. Slice chicken into pieces and fan over sauce and pasta. Serve with your choice of steamed vegetables.

1 cup canola oil

2 tablespoons garlic, minced

1/2 cup yellow onion, diced

1 cup lime juice

1 cup tequila

2 tablespoons cumin

1 tablespoon ground black pepper

1/3 cup fresh cilantro, chopped

2 1/3 teaspoons cayenne pepper (optional)

4 (8-ounce) chicken breasts, skinned and boned

4 oz butter

2/3 cup flour

4 cups half and half

12 oz whipped cream cheese

1/2 teaspoon white pepper

2 tablespoons chicken base

1/2 teaspoon salt

1 lb pasta (your favorite)

WINSLOW'S CITY MARKET BARBECUE
SINCE 1971

20 E. 5th St., Kansas City, MO (816)471-7427

One of the most famous sandwiches in Kansas City gets its notoriety because it's burnt. It's The Famous Smokie and it's only at Winslow's City Market Barbecue.

The dearly loved and top-rated burnt-end sandwich has been a Kansas City tradition for over 25 years. So don't ask for it any other way except perhaps accompanied by some of the Winslow's "killer" spicy wings, succulent slow-smoked ribs or three-time grand prize winning Chili.

Seasoned ribs slow smoked over hickory and served with a mouth watering barbecue sauce

Winslow's Famous Smoked Ribs

PrepTime: 5 minutes
Cooking Time: 240-360 minutes
Servings Per Recipe: 9

1 **Rib Rub:** Combine salt, pepper, paprika, and sugar thoroughly together. Set aside.

2 **Ribs:** Trim ribs and remove membrane that covers the underside of ribs. Apply rib rub lightly. Place in cooker/smoker.

3 Heat a smoker to 250-300° F. Winslow's uses only green hickory wood, however, water-soaked hickory chips over coals can be used. Place the slab, bone side up with the arch of the ribs at the top, in the center of the smoker. Smoke 4-6 hours. You can baste the ribs 15 minutes before serving or serve sauce on the side. Check the ribs to see if they are done by pinching the meat between the bones. If you can pinch through the rib meat then they are finished. When you cut the ribs, you should see a nice pink smoke ring around the outer edge. Enjoy!

1/4 cup salt

1/2 cup coarse black pepper

1/2 cup paprika

1/2 cup sugar

2 (3-pound) slabs of pork spare ribs

The Roasterie
AIR·ROASTED COFFEE

2601 Madison, Kansas City, MO
(816)931-4000

The Roasterie offers the best cup of coffee around, but you can't visit them. That's because they're the company that supplies special gourmet blends to grocery stores, to fine area restaurants, to local TV and radio stations for special promotions, as well as to Restaurant Secrets in promoting this book.

The Roasterie believes that gourmet coffee is as important as the right wine or the right dessert. They research exactly what best enhances their clients' cuisine: studying a restaurant's menu, its desserts, and its ambience. They even consider the time of day in which the coffee will be enjoyed. They don't stop until they unveil that unique flavor that brings customers back for more.

Danny O'Neill is the Bean Baron at the Roasterie, discovering his first coffee bean while an exchange student in Costa Rica. Try any of their coffees and you'll be able to taste and smell the difference their commitment makes.

Unique blends of coffee designed exclusively for the finest restaurants of Kansas City

Ahhhhh...Coffee!

PrepTime: 2 minutes
Cooking Time: 4-6 minutes
Servings Per Recipe: 1

1 **Clean Equipment:** As with any type of food or beverage, beginning with clean equipment is a must. Even small amounts of old coffee oil will spoil a great cup of coffee.

2 **Quality Coffee:** Similarly, fresh roasted, top quality specialty coffee is crucial to brewing great coffee at home. Stale or commercial grade coffees will disappoint every time.

3 **Quality Water:** Since the final beverage is approximately 98.2% water, it is imperative that high quality water be used. Filtered is better than non-filtered; spring water is best.

4 **Proper Grind:** Proper grind is very important as well. If the grind is too fine, the coffee will over-extract and become bitter. If the grind is too coarse, the resulting beverage will be under-extracted and thin. Always adjust your grind based on the type of coffee brewer that you use. Your local specialty coffee roaster can assist you with any questions.

5 **Proper Formula:** Many times consumers create bitter coffee by simply not using enough coffee. This results in the coffee being over-extracted..."wringing" bitterness out of overworked grounds. Always use one level coffee measure per 6 ounces of water. This ratio never changes, regardless of how many cups you are brewing.

6 **Proper Temperature:** Brewing temperature is most desirable between 194° - 204° F. Colder water will produce a flat, weak, under-extracted beverage. Hotter water will cause some of the desired organic materials to decompose and reduce optimal quality.

7 **Proper Time:** Finally, use a brewer that completes the brewing process in 4 - 6 minutes. Immediately transfer brewed coffee to an insulated, airtight holding vessel. Brew time, or dwell time, that is too short will result in under developed or flat tasting coffee. Brew times that are too long will produce a beverage that is over-extracted or bitter.

8 **DON'TS:** Use soaps or detergents to clean your coffee equipment. - Refridgerate or freeze your coffee(use an airtight container instead). - Grind your coffee more than 5 minutes prior to brewing. - Buy or use coffee that puports to stay fresh for up to 6 months. - Use distilled, soft, or water with a taste or aroma to make coffee. - Use a spinning blade coffee grinder(use a burr or mill grinder only).

Remember, the difference between a great cup of coffee and a disappointing cup of coffee is very small indeed. Likewise, the difference in beverage quality between fine Specialty Coffee and commercial grade is very small if they are poorly prepared. Life is too short to drink nasty coffee! A little practice can make you a "pro" when it comes to preparing great coffee. Enjoy the process!

Clean equipment

Quality coffee

Quality water

Proper grind

Proper formula

Proper temperature

Proper time

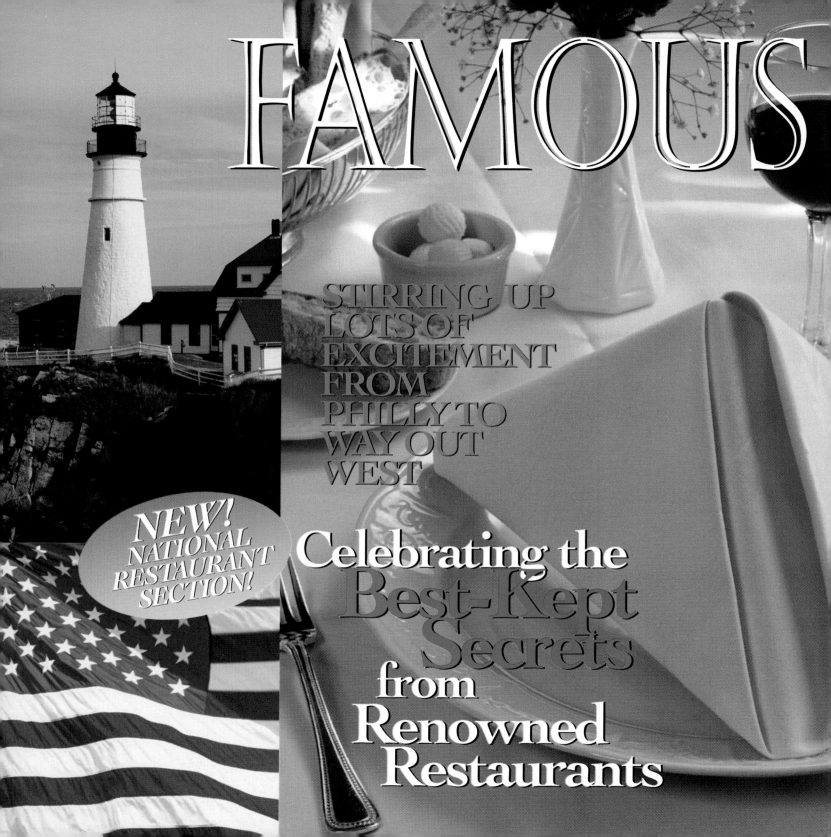

FAMOUS

STIRRING UP
LOTS OF
EXCITEMENT
FROM
PHILLY TO
WAY OUT
WEST

**NEW!
NATIONAL
RESTAURANT
SECTION!**

Celebrating the
Best-Kept
Secrets
from
Renowned
Restaurants

SECRETS

RECIPES ONLY INSIDERS KNEW (UNTIL NOW!)

Bringing our long awaited
TASTE-OF-THE-TOWN RECIPES
into your very own kitchen

Rue Bourbon

Bourbon

A Taste of Philadelphia

signature crab cake with light mustard sauce accompanied by a small green salad

Le Bec-Fin

1523 Walnut St., Philadelphia, PA (215)567-1000

Le Bec Fin has been a restaurant for memorable dining experiences since 1970. In 28 years, Chef/Owner George Perrier has made it an institution and a tradition.

Le Bec Fin offers a phenomenal six-course menu with a continuous stream of superlative dishes. Every detail is important to Chef Perrier. His dining room staff delivers impeccable service with an unusual blend of French ritual with American informality.

The hospitality industry regularly gives Le Bec Fin its highest accolades.

"5 Stars" - Mobil Travel Guide

"AAA Five Diamond Award"

Country's Highest Scoring Restaurant - Zagat

Philadelphia's "Top Table" - Gourmet Magazine

"#1 Restaurant in the Nation" - Conde Nast Traveler Magazine

"1989 Chef of the Year" - Maitres Cuisiniers de France

Galette de Crabe "Le Bec-Fin"

PrepTime: 60 minutes
Cooking Time: 15 minutes
Servings Per Recipe: 8-10

1 **Galettes:** Chill shrimp, bowl and steel "s" blade of a food processor, in the freezer for 30 minutes.

2 In a small skillet, sauté the scallions in 1 tablespoon of butter, until just wilted. Set aside to cool.

3 Place shrimp in food processor bowl fitted with the "s" blade, and puree on high speed for 1 minute or until well chopped. Using a rubber spatula, scrape down sides of bowl; add eggs and process until mixture appears smooth and shiny (about 2 minutes). With machine running, slowly pour in heavy cream. Scrape bowl and process again until cream is incorporated. Transfer shrimp mixture to a bowl; stir in mustard, Worcestershire, and Tabasco. Gently fold in cooked scallions and crab meat.

4 Place 4 or 5 (3-inch) oiled ring molds into a lightly oiled non-stick pan; fill each ring with the mixture - smoothing off the tops with a spoon. Over medium heat, cook crab cakes until golden brown (about 2 minutes on each side). Once the cakes are browned, push down rings to cut off any excess crab mixture; remove rings from around crab cakes. Remove cakes from pan. Repeat procedure until all crab mixture is used.

5 **Sauce:** In a blender or food processor, combine egg yolk, vinegar, Dijon, and chicken stock. Blend until smooth (about 30 seconds). While machine is running, drizzle in olive oil until the sauce is emulsified (creamy in appearance). Add mustard and season with salt and pepper to taste.

6 **Endive:** In a small sauté pan, heat butter and lemon juice. Add endive and sugar; toss together. Cook over medium heat until endive is wilted (but not soft) and pan juices are absorbed. Season with salt and pepper to taste, and set aside.

7 **Putting it together:** Preheat oven to 400° F. Place the crab cakes on a buttered nonstick baking pan and bake for 5 minutes or until cakes are springy to the touch. In a small pot, slowly heat the sauce over low heat - do not let it boil. Place a small amount of endive onto each plate, top with 1 or 2 crab cakes. Ladle sauce over cakes and serve immediately.

If in need of a ring mold - for small crab cakes use a round biscuit cutter, for a large one, use cleaned empty tuna can. Browned crab cakes can be refrigerated and reheated (up to 1 day).

For the Galettes:

14 oz large shrimp, peeled and deveined

1 bunch scallions, trimmed and sliced into thin rings

4 tablespoons butter (divided)

2 whole eggs, cold

2 cups heavy cream, icy cold

4 tablespoons Dijon mustard

1 tablespoon Worcestershire Sauce

1 tablespoon Tabasco Sauce

1 pound jumbo crabmeat, picked through removing any shell or cartilage

Olive oil (as needed)

For the Sauce:

1 egg yolk

1 tablespoon sherry vinegar

2 tablespoons Dijon mustard

1/2 cup chicken stock

1 1/2 cups olive oil

2 tablespoons whole-grain mustard

Salt and pepper (to taste)

For the Endive:

1 tablespoon butter

2 teaspoons lemon juice, fresh

3 heads Belgian endive, cored and cut into 1-inch lengths

1 teaspoon sugar

Salt and ground white pepper (to taste)

1 lb haricot verts (slender young green beans) trimmed and blanched (optional)

Additional Equipment:

4-5 (3-inch) ring molds

A Taste of San Francisco

A Q U A

**252 California St., San Francisco, CA
(415)956-9662**

Aqua operates out of a magnificent post-1906 earthquake building in the heart of San Francisco's bustling Financial District. Owner Charles Condy and Executive Chef Michael Mina join forces to redefine seafood dining with their elegant tribute to the flavors of the sea. Chef Mina's intensely flavorful and creative seafood cooking has earned him a reputation as one of the nation's most influential and respected chefs.

Aqua is a model for the contemporary American restaurant design, effortlessly combining a relaxed yet elegant ambiance. Through the soaring glass doors trimmed in white maple, Charles Condy's dramatic California landscape springs to life. A series of small frescoes, by notable Bay area artist Wade Hoefer, chronicle the sun's movement over the Pacific from sunrise to sunset. At the rear of the dining area there is a large fresco depicting a rosy sun dipping past the horizon of a quiet lake - a fitting conclusion to a perfect meal.

"1997 Rising Star Chef of the Year Award" - James Beard Foundation

Layered potato pancakes, minced egg, smoked salmon, horseradish crème frâiche and caviar

Caviar Parfait Tasting

PrepTime: 30 minutes
Cooking Time: 5 minutes
Servings Per Recipe: 10

1 **Potato Cakes:** Bake potatoes in 375° F oven until tender (approximately 30 minutes).

2 Grate potatoes using a hand grater. In a bowl, mix together potatoes, herbs, egg whites, salt and potato starch; mix ingredients well. Shape cakes into 2 1/2-inch diameter mold. If potato cakes are not moist enough to stick, add additional egg white.

3 In a large deep pot, add oil and heat. When oil is hot, deep fry potato cakes at 350° F until golden brown. Remove cakes to paper towels to drain, set aside momentarily.

4 **Egg Mixture:** Separate yolks and white of hard-boiled eggs and sift through a small strainer. Add parsley and minced red onion; season mixture with salt and pepper. Separate 5 tablespoons for garnish.

5 **Horseradish Crème Frâiche:** In a bowl, mix together, crème frâiche, horseradish, lemon zest, and chives; season with salt and pepper. Whip mixture until stiff.

6 **Dill Oil:** In a blender or food processor, process dill and oil; season to taste with salt and pepper.

7 **Putting it Together:** On a medium dinner plate, place potato cake in center. Using a ring mold, layer on top of potato cake - first - egg mixture, second - diced salmon, third - horseradish crème frâiche, and the top - caviar.

8 Garnish plate with remaining egg mixture and dill oil.

Ring molds can be purchased at specialty kitchen shops.

For the Potato Cake:

4 russet potatoes, scrubbed

1/2 cup fines herbes (thyme, chervil, chives and parsley)

2 egg whites

2 tablespoons salt

2 tablespoons potato starch

Vegetable oil

For the Egg Mixture:

7 eggs, hard-boiled

2 teaspoons parsley, trimmed and chopped

2 teaspoons red onion, peeled and minced

Salt and pepper (to taste)

For the Horseradish Crème Frâiche:

1 1/2 cups crème frâiche

1 teaspoon horseradish

2 teaspoons lemon zest, chopped

2 teaspoons chives, chopped

Salt and pepper (to taste)

For the Dill Oil:

1/2 bunch dill, blanched

1/2 cup canola oil

For the Caviar and Smoked Salmon:

10 oz osetra caviar

2 cups smoked salmon, diced

A Taste Of New Jersey

Huge mushrooms filled with squash puree, wrapped in phyllo & topped with Balsamic Syrup

RAM'S HEAD INN
Country Cozy Dining

9 West White Horse Pike, Absecon, NJ
(609)652-1700

Ram's Head Inn is a beautiful restaurant set on five country acres with sprawling gardens and flower-lined fences. Just eight miles from the bustling Atlantic City casinos, its wood-burning fireplaces and soft candlelight provide a respite for the senses and enhance the dining rooms.

Guests at Ram's Head Inn have a chance to enjoy quiet, distinctive country dining in an elegant and cozy atmosphere. Cocktails and other beverages can be enjoyed in the Gallery or in the Tavern by the fireplace.

Executive Chef Luigi Baretto has trained and worked throughout Europe.

AAA Four Diamond Award

DiRoNA Award

Phyllo Purse of Portabella Mushrooms

PrepTime: 60 minutes
Cooking Time: 70 minutes
Servings Per Recipe: 1-4

1 **Squash Puree:** Preheat oven to 400° F. Cut squash lengthwise in half; remove seeds. Place cut side down on an oiled baking sheet. Roast in oven for 1 hour, or until tender. Remove outer shell; in a food processor, puree pulp with butter. Season with salt, pepper, and nutmeg, to taste. Fold in almonds and set aside.

2 **Mushrooms:** In a nonreactive container, add 1/2 cup olive oil, garlic, parsley, salt, and pepper. Coat the mushrooms in the marinade; let mushrooms marinate for 30 minutes. Lower oven temperature to 350° F, place marinated mushrooms in an oven-proof dish; roast in oven until tender, approximately 10-15 minutes.

3 **Balsamic Reduction:** In a saucepot, combine balsamic vinegar and port wine. Bring to a simmer and reduce to 1 cup or until syrupy consistency is reached (approximately 20 minutes). Adjust seasonings with salt and pepper, to taste.

4 **Putting it Together:** Generously spread butternut squash puree onto stem side of mushrooms. Lay one sheet of phyllo onto a clean surface. Brush with melted butter. Lay the second sheet of phyllo on top and brush again with butter; top with last sheet of phyllo. Divide sheets into 4 equal squares. Place filled mushroom caps atop each square. Fold phyllo dough to encase mushroom to form into a purse. Place on a baking sheet and bake at 350° F for 10 minutes (or until golden brown). Paint plate with balsamic syrup (reduction) and top with mushrooms. Garnish with julienned peppers and serve.

For the Squash:

1 butternut squash

Salt and pepper (to taste)

Nutmeg (to taste)

4 tablespoons butter

2 tablespoons toasted sliced almonds

For the Mushrooms:

1/2 cup olive oil

Salt and pepper (to taste)

1 tablespoon garlic, chopped

1 teaspoon parsley, chopped

4 medium to large Portabella mushrooms, cleaned

For the Balsamic Reduction:

3 cups balsamic vinegar

1 cup port wine

For the Phyllo:

3 sheets phyllo dough

8 tablespoons butter, melted

For the Garnish:

1/2 red pepper, seeded, deveined and cut into fine julienne

1/2 green pepper, seeded, deveined and cut into fine julienne

1/2 yellow pepper, seeded, deveined and cut into fine julienne

An appetizer with an Asian flair - seafood potstickers with sake dip and hot mustard sauce

dahlia lounge

1904 - 4th Ave., Seattle, WA (206)682-4142

A visit to Seattle wouldn't be complete without a visit to the Dahlia Lounge, Chef Tom Douglas' stylish and inventive restaurant.

Located in the heart of the city, the award-winning Dahlia Lounge serves the finest in Northwest cuisine. Chef Douglas and his talented kitchen crew bring imaginative specialties to your table in a setting that is whimsical, warm and inviting. Please visit their website. (www.tomdouglas.com)

"Seattle's Quintessential and Most Creative Restaurant"
- Food and Wine Magazine

Lobster and Shiitake Potstickers

PrepTime: 60 minutes

Cooking Time: 10 minutes

Servings Per Recipe: 6-8

1 Puree lobster and shrimp meat in food processor until smooth. In a skillet, sauté shiitake mushrooms and carrots in a little of the peanut oil until softened; allow to cool. In a large mixing bowl, combine pureed lobster and shrimp, sautéed shiitakes and carrots, sesame seeds, green onion, cilantro, garlic, and garlic-chili paste. Mix thoroughly.

2 To form potstickers, lay a wrapper down on wax paper. Wet the edges of the wrapper with an index finger dipped in water. Place one tablespoon of the filling in the center of the wrapper and bring two opposing points of the wrapper together to form a triangle. Press the edges together, making a series of small creases along the edges. Refrigerate until all potstickers are assembled.

3 In a large pot, bring 1 gallon of water to boil over high heat. Add potstickers, a few dozen at a time, and cook for 5-8 minutes. When ready, they should float to the surface of the water. Using a small sieve or mesh skimmer, gently scoop potstickers out of the water, being careful not to break them. Continue until all potstickers are poached.

4 Heat about 2 tablespoons of oil in a 10-inch non-stick sauté pan over medium heat. Pan-fry the potstickers in batches (no more than 10 at a time), browning on both sides. Keep warm until all potstickers have been pan-fried, using more oil as needed.

5 **Sake Dip:** In a small pan, combine sake, soy sauce, vinegar, chili, garlic, ginger, and sugar. Warm gently until sugar has dissolved. Remove from heat, cool, then add green onion.

6 **Hot Mustard:** In a small bowl, combine dry mustard with water to form a paste. Mix in soy sauce, rice wine vinegar, honey, sesame oil, and sesame seeds. Add more water if needed to make a nice dipping consistency.

7 **Putting it Together:** Serve potstickers with lime wedges, sake dip, and hot mustard.

For the Pot Stickers:

2/3 lb raw lobster meat

1/3 lb raw shrimp meat

1 1/2 cups shiitake mushrooms, cleaned and thinly sliced

1/3 cup carrots, peeled and finely diced

1 tablespoon toasted sesame seeds

1 tablespoon green onion, trimmed and very finely chopped

1 tablespoon cilantro, finely chopped

1/2 teaspoon garlic, peeled and minced

2 teaspoons Chinese garlic-chili paste

40 wonton or gyoza wrappers

Peanut or vegetable oil for (sautéing)

For the Sake Dip:

1/2 cup sake

1/4 cup soy sauce

1/4 cup rice wine vinegar

1 small serrano chili, seeded and chopped

1/4 teaspoon minced garlic

1/4 teaspoon fresh ginger, peeled and minced

1 tablespoon sugar

1 tablespoon green onion, finely chopped

For the Hot Mustard:

1/4 cup dry hot mustard

1/3 cup water, or as needed

2 tablespoons soy sauce

2 tablespoons rice wine vinegar

2 teaspoons honey

1 teaspoon sesame oil

1 tablespoon toasted sesame seeds

Crisp chilled shrimp accompanied by a zesty Asian-flavored shrimp sauce

the Tillerman

2245 E. Flamingo, Las Vegas, NV (702)731-4024

For 20 years, The Tillerman has been known as Home of the Freshest Seafood in Las Vegas - Select Alaskan King Crab Legs, Australian Lobster Tails and Maine Lobster with Angel Hair Pasta, to name just a few of their offerings. Their menu also features delicious steak, chicken and lamb dishes.

The Tillerman's large Garden Room is filled with live ficus trees, plants and an incredible retractable skylight that opens to expose the brilliance of the stars in the night sky.

Timeless comfort, a unique atmosphere, great service and an award-winning wine list, The Tillerman is sure to make your evening a night to remember.

"Top 5 Restaurants-1998" - Wine Spectator

"Best Seafood Restaurant-1998" - Las Vegas Review Journal

Asian Shrimp Cocktail

PrepTime: 10 minutes
Cooking Time: 6 minutes
Servings Per Recipe: 4

1 **Sauce:** In a mixing bowl, combine with a whisk - dry mustard, and vinegar. Add the soy sauce, honey, ginger, garlic, both oils, and green onion; combine well and chill.

2 **Shrimp:** In a large pot, combine water, onion, peppercorns, and bay leaves; bring to a boil.

3 Add shrimp to water and cook until they are firm and appear orange in color. Strain in a colander and cover them in ice to stop the cooking process. Once cool, peel shrimp and run a sharp knife down the back to devein them. Chill to very cold.

4 **Putting it Together:** Place napa cabbage on plate, top with chilled shrimp and serve with a side cup of sauce. Garnish with a lime wedge and a cilantro sprig.

For the Sauce:

1/3 cup dry mustard

1/3 cup rice wine vinegar

1/2 cup soy sauce

1/2 cup honey

1 tablespoon fresh ginger, peeled and finely grated

1 teaspoon fresh garlic, peeled and finely chopped

1/3 cup sesame oil

1 3/4 cup peanut oil

1/8 cup green onions, thinly sliced

For the Shrimp:

1 gallon water

1 small yellow onion peeled

1 tablespoon black peppercorns

2 bay leaves

20 large raw shrimp (shelled)

Garnish:

Napa cabbage

Lime wedge(s)

Cilantro Sprigs

A Taste Of Manhattan

Wild and flavorful - this mushroom soup is the perfect first course or light entrée

---

TAVERN ON THE GREEN

**CENTRAL PARK AT WEST 67TH ST.,
NEW YORK, NY (212)873-3200**

Tavern on the Green is a grand café overlooking Central Park. It is a genuine showstopper, overflowing with crystal chandeliers, hand-carved mirrors and stained glass. Critics say, "If Oz had a restaurant, this would be it!"

Tavern on the Green is open seven days a week, 365 days a year. Located on New York's Upper West Side, it is just three blocks from Lincoln Center and a quick cab ride to Carnegie Hall and Broadway.

Constructed to house sheep in 1870, the building became a restaurant in 1934. In 1974, Warner LeRoy, who revolutionized the American dining scene with his legendary Maxwell's Plum, took over the restaurant and embarked upon a $10 million renovation, which became Tavern on the Green.

From the moment it opened on August 31, 1976, the reinvigorated Tavern took New York by storm, dazzling the city with its decorative setting, eclectic menus and all-around playfulness.

Sam Hazen's Harvest Wild Mushroom Soup

PrepTime: 15 minutes
Cooking Time: 45 minutes
Servings Per Recipe: 4

1 Slice and stem all domestic and criminis; reserve the stems, slice fennel. Reserve tops of fennel. Slice onion.

2 In a heavy bottom pot, gently sauté onions, fennel, domestic and crimini mushrooms in unsalted butter. Do not brown mixture until fennel is tender.

3 During this time (in a bowl), toss shiitakes and Portobellos in oil, thyme, salt, pepper, and chopped garlic. Lay out on baking sheets and roast in 350° F oven until golden brown.

4 In a pot, place reserved mushroom stems and fennel tops in chicken broth and allow to infuse over medium heat, then remove.

5 Remove baking sheet from oven; discard thyme and garlic. Place browned mushrooms into soup pot; add potatoes after slicing thin. At this point, all mushrooms, fennel slices, and onions should be in one pot. Add broth. Simmer until potato is fully cooked.

6 Remove soup from heat source and purée in blender or food processor (process in small batches). Adjust seasoning with salt and pepper. Finish soup with truffle oil and porcini powder.

Truffle oil and porcini powder can be purchased at specialty food shops.

2 cups shiitake mushrooms, cleaned and stemmed (stems reserved)

2 cups Portobello mushrooms, cleaned and stemmed (stems and gills reserved)

4 cups crimini mushrooms, cleaned, stemmed (stems reserved) and sliced

1 cup domestic mushrooms, cleaned and sliced (stems reserved)

2 large onions, peeled and sliced

2 heads of fennel (tops reserved), sliced

1/2 stick unsalted butter (for sautéeing)

2 whole russet potatoes, peeled

1 quart chicken broth (homemade or prepared)

1 bunch fresh thyme

1/4 cup garlic, peeled and chopped

Salt and pepper (as needed)

Truffle oil (to garnish)

Porcini powder (to garnish)

Pear salad with tiny beans, rice wine vinaigrette, honey crusted almonds and scallops

SALAMANDER
RESTAURANT

1 Athenaeum St., Cambridge, MA (617)225-2121

A renovated Cambridge ink factory is the backdrop for Chef/Owner Stan Frankenthaler's innovative Asian-tinged cuisine. Since its opening, only three short years ago, Salamander has been recognized by every major publication in the country; the Boston Globe proclaimed it "a four-star restaurant in the making." As soon as you enter the gracious dining room with exposed kitchen the aromas of the wood-burning hearth excite your senses. The restaurant showcases works by local artists, as well as fruits, produce, and cheeses grown and produc locally. The chef's signature dish of lightly fried lobster with lemongrass, ginger and Thai basil highlights the ever-changing menu of seasonal specialties available. Two private rooms, an attentive/knowledgeable staff, an an award-winning wine list are all part of why Travel and Leisure says this is "the one not to miss". Just minutes from downtown Boston, Salamander is decidedl worth seeking out. Reservations are recommended, walk-ins always welcomed.

Asian Pear Salad with Pear Glazed Scallops

PrepTime: 20 minutes
Cooking Time: 10 minutes
Servings Per Recipe: 4

1 **Salad:** In a pot of boiling water, blanch the haricot vert and reserve. Wash all greens well; trim and cut frisée in half and reserve along with the haricot vert, peppers and pears.

2 **Vinaigrette:** In a bowl, whisk together shallots, ginger, rice vinegar, mirin, pear nectar, both oils, salt and pepper.

3 **Almonds:** In a sauce pan, caramelize honey; add in coriander and chili flakes - then stir in almonds. Remove from heat, quickly separate almonds onto an oiled baking sheet (to avoid clumping); allow almonds to cool.

4 **Scallops:** Clean the scallops and reserve. Prepare the glaze - in a small sauce pan, combine sugar, water, ginger, and pickling spice; reduce to a thick syrup and strain into pear nectar.

5 **Putting it Together:** In one sauté pan, season and sear the frisée; toss in remaining greens, haricot vert, peppers and the vinaigrette. Season with salt and pepper, toss and remove to serving plates. In a second sauté pan (heat to hot), season and sear the scallops; glaze them and arrange on salad.

6 Garnish with honey-spice almonds and serve.

For the Salad:
1/4 pound haricot vert (slender young green beans)
1 sweet red pepper, seeded, deveined and julienned
4 small heads frisée (a variety of endive)
1/4 pound mizuna
1/4 pound baby spinach, washed well and trimmed
1 head radicchio
2 Asian pears (other varieties may be substituted) and julienned

For the Vinaigrette:
1 shallot, peeled and minced
1 tablespoon ginger, peeled and minced
3 tablespoons rice vinegar
1 tablespoon mirin (sweet rice wine)
2 tablespoons pear nectar
2 tablespoons sesame oil
1/4 cup canola oil
Salt and pepper (to taste)

For the Almonds:
1/2 cup honey
1 teaspoon ground coriander
1 teaspoon ground chili flakes
1 cup toasted whole almonds

For the Scallops:
8-12 ounces pristine scallops
1/4 cup sugar
1/4 cup water
1 slice fresh ginger (peeled)
1 tablespoons pickling spice
1/4 cup pear nectar
Salt and pepper (to taste)

A Taste Of New Orleans

Beef filet grilled to perfection and topped with a red wine sauce & a horseradish sauce

Brennan's®

417 Royal St., New Orleans, LA (504)525-9711

Dining out in New Orleans would not be complete without a visit to the world famous Brennan's Restaurant. Breakfast at Brennan's is a tradition for local New Orleanians and visitors from all parts of the globe. Brennan's is also recognized for its outstanding lunches and dinners.

Founded by Owen Jr., Jimmy and Ted Brennan, the restaurant is located in the historic Murphy House, a pink stucco mansion at 417 Royal Street in the heart of the French Quarter. Brennan's is noted for its lush courtyard and elegant intimate dining rooms - 12 in all.

Southern hospitality is dispensed at Brennan's on a grand scale and Brennan's 50,000-bottle wine cellar has been repeatedly recognized by the Wine Spectator as one of the most outstanding in the world.

"Grand Award" - Wine Spectator

Travel Holiday Magazine Dining Award yearly since 1956

"Top Five Restaurants of New Orleans" - Zagat Survey

Filet Stanley

PrepTime: 15-20 minutes
Cooking Time: 10-15 minutes
Servings Per Recipe: 8

1 **Brennan's Red Wine Mushroom Sauce:** In a large saucepan or Dutch oven, melt the butter. Add onion and sauté for several minutes, until tender. Stir in the tomato paste, mushrooms and paprika. Cook until the mushrooms are tender; add the flour. Stir the mixture until well blended, then using a whisk, incorporate the beef stock. When sauce is smooth, add scallions, Worcestershire, wine, and garlic. Season with salt and pepper to taste. Simmer about 25 minutes, serve warm with steaks.

2 **Horseradish Sauce:** In a saucepan, combine cream, pepper, and salt. Cook over medium heat (do not let the cream reach a boil). Blend the butter and flour together, and form a small ball. Add butter ball to the simmering cream. Cook until sauce is smooth; add horseradish. Serve warm with steaks.

3 **Filet Stanley:** Prepare a grill or broiler. Sprinkle the halved steaks on both sides with salt and pepper. Grill or broil meat to desired doneness.

4 In a large skillet, melt butter and sauté sliced bananas until tender and lightly browned (approximately 4 minutes per side).

5 **Putting it Together:** Place 2 Holland rusks in the center of 8 heated plates. Arrange a slice of banana on either side of the rusks (near edge of plate). Spoon horseradish sauce between the bananas and the rusks. Place a cooked filet on each Holland rusk and top with Brennan's Red Wine Mushroom Sauce.

Suggested accompaniments: fresh baked french bread & butter, Cabernet Sauvignon.

For the Brennan's Red Wine and Mushroom Sauce: Yields 3 cups

1/2 cup butter (1 stick)
1 cup onion, peeled and diced
1/2 cup tomato paste
2 cups sliced mushrooms
1 1/2 tablespoons paprika
1/4 cup all-purpose flour
3 cups beef stock (homemade or prepared)
2 cups scallions, trimmed and sliced
1 tablespoon Worcestershire Sauce
3/4 cup Burgundy wine
1 tablespoon minced garlic
Salt and pepper (to taste)

For the Horseradish Sauce: Yields 1 1/2 cups

2 cups heavy cream
1/4 teaspoon white pepper
1/4 teaspoon salt
1/4 teaspoon butter
2 tablespoons all-purpose flour
2 tablespoons horseradish

For the Filet Stanley:

8 beef filets, (8-ounces each), halved
Salt and freshly ground black pepper (to taste)
1/2 cup butter
8 bananas, peeled and sliced in half lengthwise
16 Holland rusks (Zwieback toast-like bread)
1/2 cup horseradish sauce (see recipe)
2 cups Brennan's Red Wine and Mushroom Sauce (see recipe)

A Taste Of Manhattan

A unique appetizer with an Asian flair

THE FOUR SEASONS

99 E. 52nd St., New York, NY (212)754-9494

Not to be confused with the hotel chain with a similar name, The Four Seasons is a world-class restaurant designed in 1959 by Phillip Johnson, one of this century's finest architects.

Located in the Seagram Building on Park Avenue, The Four Seasons is one of the city's most glamourous restaurants. During lunch it plays host to movers and shakers in the worlds of politics, finance, and publishing. When the lights go down, the restaurant becomes an irresistably romantic place to enjoy the most delicious wines and foods, like the Crisp Nori Tuna with Blood Orange Miso Sauce pictured here.

Crisp Nori Tuna with Blood Orange Miso Sauce

PrepTime: 10 minutes
Cooking Time: 10 minutes
Servings Per Recipe: 2

1 **Tuna:** Clean and trim tuna into cylindrical shape. Spread wasabi paste on tuna to season.

2 Lay out nori wrapper and put on julienned vegetables, top with tuna and roll (like sushi); seal with tempura flour mix.

3 Dip tuna into tempura flour mix until well coated; roll tuna into panko crumbs until well coated.

4 **Sauce:** In a sauce pan, reduce orange juice with ginger, shallots, and garlic until it becomes a glaze. Add sambal to taste. Set aside and cool strain mixture. Whisk in grapeseed oil and miso paste. Season with salt and pepper to taste.

5 **Final Preparation and Putting it Together:** In a skillet or wok, add oil and deep fry panko-coated tuna roll until golden brown (do not over-fry). Tuna should be cooked medium-rare.

6 Cut tuna roll into four pieces. Garnish with enoki mushrooms, pea shoot sprouts and blood orange segments (optional).

Wasabi, panko, nori wrapper, enoki mushrooms, and pea shoots are all available at Asian markets and some specialty food shops.

8 ounces sushi-grade bluefin tuna

1 teaspoon wasabi paste (Japanese horseradish)

1 dried nori wrapper

1/2 cup carrots, zucchini, and yellow squash, julienned and blanched

1/2 cup tempura flour mix (for coating and frying)

Panko (Japanese bread crumbs)

1/2 cup blood orange juice

1/2 teaspoon ginger root, peeled and roughly chopped

1/2 teaspoon shallots, peeled and roughly chopped

1/2 teaspoon garlic, peeled and roughly chopped

Sambal (chile-based seasoning)

3 tablespoons grapeseed oil

2 tablespoons miso paste

Salt and pepper (to taste)

Vegetable oil (for frying)

For the Garnish:

Enoki mushrooms

Pea shoot sprouts

Blood orange segments

A Taste Of Boston

A light and delicious Cambodian chicken dish - serve with Jasmine Rice

THE ELEPHANT WALK
FRENCH AND CAMBODIAN CUISINE

900 Beacon St., Boston, MA
(617)247-1500

2067 Mass Ave., Cambridge, MA
(617)492-6900

The first of two Elephant Walk restaurants opened in Union Square, Somerville in August 1991. Overwhelming success of their innovative French Cambodian Cuisine and critical acclaim led to the opening of a second Elephant Walk on Beacon Street in Boston in 1994, and a Cambodian Tapas-style restaurant in Waltham in December 1997.

Located just minutes from historic Fenway Park, the Elephant Walk on Beacon Street attracts gourmands from all walks of life, a clientele as diverse as their menu. Specialties include Rare Pan Seared Tuna Loin Over Spiced Red and Green Chili Cream Sauce.

The Somerville restaurant was recently moved to Massachusetts Avenue in Porter Square, Cambridge. The Elephant Walk owner/operators, Longteine and Kenthao de Monteiro, continually strive to provide a combination of the best Cambodian and French culinary traditions.

Lemongrass Chicken

PrepTime: 195 minutes
Cooking Time: 10 minutes
Servings Per Recipe: 4

1 **Stock:** In a stockpot, simmer bones, onion, carrots, celery, and bay leaves in 1 1/2 gallons water for 3 hours

2 **Lemongrass Paste:** Lightly chop lemongrass, galangal, lime leaf, garlic, shallot, cilantro and turmeric. In a food processor (or blender), puree with 1/4 cup water until smooth.

3 **Chicken:** Remove cartilage from breast meat and cut into 1/2-inch strips. In a medium-hot sauté pan, sear chicken on all sides. Add sugar, salt, onion, pepper and scallion; sauté for 2 minutes. Gradually add 1/4 cup chicken stock and 3 teaspoons lemongrass paste; simmer mixture to sauce consistency.

Crushed red pepper may be added for a spicy flavor addition.

For the Chicken Stock:

5 lb bones, to simmer in 1 1/2 gallons water for 3 hours

1 cup onion, peeled and diced

1 cup carrots, peeled and chopped

1 cup celery, chopped

2 bay leaves

For the Lemongrass Paste:

2 stalks lemongrass (discard outer leaves, root, and tip)

1 tablespoon galangal, peeled and chopped

1 kaffir lime leaf (center vein removed)

2 tablespoons garlic, peeled and chopped

1 tablespoon shallot, peeled and chopped

1/4 cup cilantro leaves

1/2 teaspoon turmeric

For the Chicken:

4 (6-ounce) chicken breasts, boned and cut into 1/2-inch pieces

3 teaspoons sugar (or to taste)

1 teaspoon salt (or to taste)

Spanish onion, peeled and cut into small julienne

Red pepper, seeded deveined and cut into small julienne

Scallions, trimmed and cut into small julienne

Chopped peanuts (for garnish)

Orange roughy filets wrapped in potatoes and accompanied by Sweet & Sour Tomato Sauce

BERNARD'S

506 S. Grand Ave., Los Angeles , CA
(213)612-1580

Bernard's at the historic Regal Biltmore Hotel is located off Rendezvous Court. Bernard's award-winning Continental Cuisine features an epicurean selection of grilled seafood and meats in an elegant wood-panelled setting.

Only minutes away from the Music Center, Bernard's offers the perfect location for pre-theater dining or a romantic evening getaway for two. Bernard's has been the recipient of numerous awards including being voted among the "Top 50" restaurants in the nation by readers of Condé Nast Traveler, and voted among the "Top 20" restaurants in Los Angeles by Gourmet Magazine's reader survey.

The menu, under the guidance of Executive Chef Roger Pigozzi, features Continental Cuisine with an emphasis on fresh fish, seafood and game. In addition, Bernard's offers the "Chef's Table," a special menu prepared by Chef Pigozzi and served in the legendary Regal Biltmore kitchen for groups of as many as 40. At 25,000 square feet, the kitchen is one of the largest in Los Angeles.

Orange Roughy Wrapped in Potatoes

PrepTime: 10 minutes
Cooking Time: 20 minutes
Servings Per Recipe: 4

1 Season the potatoes and fish with salt and pepper, to taste. Heat oil in saucepan over medium heat, until hot. Place a layer of grated potatoes in the saucepan; add a thin piece of fish filet on top. Place another thin layer of potatoes on top of fish. Cook on one side until golden brown (approximately 5 minutes over medium heat). When first side is done, carefully turn and cook on other side. When done, transfer to warm serving dish making sure excess oil has been drained. Complete the procedure with remaining fish.

2 **Sauce:** In a saucepan, caramelize the sugar. Add vinegar and boil for 3 minutes. Add tomato juice and clam juice and return to a boil. Continue to boil for an additional 3 minutes. Adjust seasonings with salt and pepper.

2 pounds orange roughy, filets

4 large potatoes, peeled and grated to fine julienne

2 cups salad oil

3 teaspoons salt (or to taste)

1 teaspoon white pepper (or to taste)

For the Sauce:

1 tablespoon sugar

1/2 cup balsamic vinegar

1 cup tomato juice

1/2 cup clam juice

Salt and pepper (to taste)

A Taste of Miami

This zesty grouper has a hint of saffron and is accompanied by flavorful plantains

NEW WORLD CUISINE

CHEF ALLEN'S

19088 N.E. 29th Avenue, Aventura, FL
(305)935-2900

Chef Allen's Restaurant specializes in New World cuisine. The award-winning restaurant's menu changes daily and features fresh local fish and tropical fruits and vegetables.

Their signature dish is the souffle and they offer an array of interesting and different selections, one for each night of the week.

An excellent and extensive wine list, including a wide selection of wines by the glass, perfectly complements the menu.

"Award of Excellence" - The Wine Spectator

"Best Wine by the Glass in Miami" - Food and Wine Magazine

"Ponce de Leon" - New World Cuisine

"Best Chef in the Southeastern United States" - The James Beard Foundation

Mustard Seed Crusted Grouper with Plantains

PrepTime: 25 minutes
Cooking Time: 60 minutes
Servings Per Recipe: 4

1 **Plantains:** Preheat the oven to 325°F. Coat the plantains lightly with 1 teaspoon of olive oil. In an oven-proof dish, roast the plantains for 1 hour (until soft). Remove from oven.

2 When plantains are cool enough to handle, peel and slice on the bias (1-inch thick). Sprinkle generously with brown sugar, peanuts, freshly squeezed lime juice and rum; keep warm.

3 **Sauce:** In a medium sauce pan, combine the saffron, orange juice, mustard, and Sauterne. Over medium heat, simmer sauce until reduced by half. Remove from heat source and keep warm.

4 **Grouper:** In a heavy bottomed sauce pan, warm olive oil. Season the grouper with pepper and salt, then liberally press the mustard seed onto the fish. In a skillet, pan fry the grouper, browning both sides (about 2-3 minutes per side) until cooked through.

5 **Putting it Together:** Pour the sauce in the center of each plate. Place the plantains on sauce. Place the grouper on top, and garnish with fresh cilantro.

For the Plantains:

4 medium yellow plantains

1/3 cup olive oil

1/4 cup brown sugar

1/4 cup salted roasted peanuts, chopped

Juice of 1 lime

2 tablespoons spiced rum

For the Sauce:

1/8 teaspoon saffron threads

1/2 cup fresh orange juice

1 teaspoon coarse grain mustard

2/3 cup Sauterne

For the Grouper:

4 (6-ounce) grouper filets

1 teaspoon cracked black peppercorns

1 tablespoon kosher salt

2 tablespoons black mustard seeds

3 tablespoons cilantro, chopped

A Taste Of Orange County

This doubled process smoked filet is elegant and exotic

FIVE FEET
CONTEMPORARY ·· CHINESE ·· CUISINE

328 Glenneyre St., Laguna Beach, CA
(949)497-4955

With its sandy beaches and rocky cliffs, the seaside village of Laguna Beach has long been a favorite destination for those seeking a break from the busy world

Laguna Beach is also well known as an artist colony, and lately, a certain Laguna Beach restaurant has been gaining recognition in its own right. The Five Feet restaurant, playing off the Laguna Beach's artist colony theme, has created an art gallery setting and exhibition kitchen. Here, celebrated Chef Michael Kang prepares contemporary Chinese cuisine.

Five Feet has been consistently rated with the top restaurants by Zagat and has received rave reviews from The New York Times, Los Angeles Times and Gourmet Magazine.

Winner, Gourmet Magazine National Cook-Off

"Gold Award" Southern California Restaurant Writers

"Award of Excellence" California Restaurant Writers

James Beard Foundation Award

Twice Cooked Prime Filet

PrepTime: 120 minutes
Cooking Time: 30 minutes
Servings Per Recipe: 4

1 **Marinade**: In a large container, mix together water, soy sauce, mushrooms, ginger, whiskey, peppercorns, onion, dry chile, brown sugar, vinegar, white pepper, sesame oil and star anise. Submerge filet completely in marinade; leave to marinate for 2 hours (do not exceed the 2 hour limit). Remove filet from marinade and pat dry. Place in refrigerator.

2 Remove filet from refrigerator 1 hour prior to smoking to bring beef temperature even with room temperatures (except for extremely hot days).

3 **Tea Smoking**: Prepare wok - place aluminum foil or wax paper onto bottom of wok. Place uncooked rice on top of foil or paper to weight it down.

4 In a bowl, mix together star anise, Szechuan peppercorns, jasmine tea, brown sugar and chiles. Spread evenly the mixed ingredients over foil or wax paper. Place wire rack on top of dry ingredients. Place marinated filet on wire rack; cover with plate or lid that will fit inside of wok. Place damp towel around lid to keep smoke from escaping.

5 Smoke with flame for 10 minutes. Turn off flame and let smoke for 10 more minutes. Place filet into freezer immediately to cool. One half hour prior to serving, set oven for 375° F. Roast filet for 10 minutes; let filet rest for 10 minutes before slicing and serving.

6 **Chow Chow**: In a large bowl, mix together mango, papaya, red and green onions, cilantro, basil, ginger, mint, jalapeño, honey, fish sauce, vinegar, hot oil, lemon and lime juice, and salt (to taste). Mix well; set aside in refrigerator. Spoon over filet before serving.

Additional equipment needed: wok and wire rack.

3 pounds filet of beef tenderloin (ask butcher for châteaubriand cut)

For the Filet Marinade:

1/2 quart water
1 quart soy sauce
1 cup mushrooms, cleaned and chopped
3 strips ginger root, peeled and smashed
1 cup Chinese whiskey (or cream sherry)
2 tablespoons Szechuan peppercorns, burned
1 bunch green onion, trimmed and cut into lengthy strips
10 dry chiles (or to taste)
1 cup brown sugar (rock sugar)
1/2 cup black vinegar
1 teaspoon white pepper
1/2 cup sesame oil
10 whole star anise

For the Smoking Ingredients:

1 cup rice (uncooked)
5 whole star anise
1 tablespoon Szechuan peppercorns
2 tablespoons jasmine tea
1/2 pound brown sugar
6-8 dried chiles (or to taste)

For the Asian Mango Papaya Chow Chow:

8 oz each: mango and papaya (medium diced)
1/2 medium red onion, peeled and diced
2 green onions, trimmed and chopped
1 tablespoon cilantro, chopped
1 tablespoon fresh basil, chopped (use Thai basil if possible)
1/2 teaspoon fresh ginger, peeled and minced
1/2 teaspoon fresh mint, minced
1 red jalapeño pepper, diced
2 tablespoons honey
1 tablespoon fish sauce
1 teaspoon rice vinegar
1/2 teaspoon hot oil (or to taste)
Juice of 1 lemon and 1 lime
Salt (to taste)

A Taste Of Chicago

429 Temple, Highland Park, IL
(847)432-0770

With its comfortable, understated elegance, Carlos' has earned a reputation as a wonderful place to celebrate special occasions like birthdays and anniversaries.

Located in a small, charming building in Highland Park, the intimate and romantic restaurant has been delighting patrons for 17 years with such Contemporary French dishes as Roulade of Dover Sole with Crayfish Chanterelles or Oven Roasted Fig-Glazed California Squab. And, there's always an excellent wine selection from Carlos' award-winning wine list to accompany any entree.

"Grand Award" - Wine Spectator

DiRoNA Award

"Four Stars" - Chicago Magazine

4 Stars - Chicago Tribune

Zagat Survey

Gourmet Magazine

North Shore Magazine

Food & Wine Magazine, One of the Top 25 Restaurants in North America

WBBM Radio 20 out of 20

Mobil Award - Four Diamonds

Dover sole served with crayfish, chanterelles, and sprouts in a lobster basil emulsion

Roulade of Dover Sole

PrepTime: 60 minutes

Cooking Time: 10 minutes

Servings Per Recipe: 4

1 **Filling:** In a food processor fitted with the steel "s" blade, combine 3/4 cup crayfish, butter, garlic, chipotle powder, cream, Armagnac, tarragon, basil, mint, corn flake crumbs, breadcrumbs, salt and pepper; pulse to puree and combine thoroughly (do not let mixture get too soft by over-processing). When smooth, add remaining crayfish and pulse briefly to shred and combine, leave meat visible.

2 Lay flattened filets skin side up, thinly spread filling mixture evenly over each. Starting from the tail, carefully roll each filet (making roulade) and pin with 2 toothpicks evenly spaced to hold filet secure. Place on a plate, cover, and refrigerate until ready to use.

3 **Sauce:** In a 2-quart sauce pot, lightly sauté shallot and garlic in minimum amount of oil. Add stock and cream; reduce by three-fourths (until sauce lightly coats the back of a spoon). Remove from heat, add basil and season with salt and pepper to taste. Before serving, strain through a chinois (fine mesh strainer) and skim any fat that may rise to surface. Keep warm in a warm water bath until ready to use or refrigerate overnight and reheat gently.

4 **Vegetables:** In a medium-size sauté pan, heat oil to sauté and lightly brown delicata squash. Add mushrooms, Brussels sprouts and seasonings; heat thoroughly. Add butter if mixture seems dry - then add shallots and chives and continue to heat. When ready to serve, add sprouts and toss frequently over heat. When sprouts are warmed but still crisp, check seasoning and adjust if necessary. Divide evenly among 4 plates.

5 **Final Preparation and Putting it Together:** Preheat oven to 400° F and turn broiler on. Heat large non-stick oven-ready sauté pan over medium-heat; add oil. Place roulades in pan standing on end and sauté until lightly browned. Turn over and place in oven for 3 minutes.

6 Remove pan from oven and take fish out of pan and place on cutting board. With a sharp knife, cut each roulade into 2 rounds in between the toothpicks. Place rounds on a lightly buttered pan and place under broiler for about 1 minute or until lightly browned but still very moist. Remove from pan, carefully remove toothpicks, place 4 rounds on a bed of vegetable mixture and spoon sauce around.

2 fresh Dover sole, fileted and slightly pounded thin (8 filets)

For the Filling:

1 cup cooked crayfish tails, cooled

3/4 cup unsalted butter, slightly softened

1 teaspoon roasted garlic puree

1/2 teaspoon chipotle powder

1/4 cup heavy cream

1/8 cup Armagnac (French brandy)

1/2 teaspoon minced fresh tarragon

1/2 teaspoon minced fresh basil

1/2 teaspoon minced fresh mint

1/2 cup corn flake crumbs

1/4 cup plain breadcrumbs

Salt and pepper (to taste)

For the Sauce:

1 shallot, roughly chopped

2 cloves of garlic, peeled and smashed

1 tablespoon olive oil

3 cups reduced lobster stock

1 cup heavy cream

Basil leaves and stems

For the Vegetables:

1/2 cup delicata squash, diced, blanched and cooled

Olive oil

1/2 cup chanterelle mushroom, cleaned and cut into small pieces, sautéed, seasoned and cooled

1/2 cup Brussels sprouts, blanched, cooled, and sliced into rounds

2 tablespoons butter (to sauté and reheat)

1 tablespoon minced shallots

1 tablespoon minced chives

1/2 cup pea or daikon sprouts, cut into 1-inch length

1/2 cup radish sprouts

Salt and white pepper (to taste)

Additional Equipment:

Toothpicks

L'Auberge Chez François

332 Springvale Rd., Great Falls, VA (703)759-380(

Alsace-Lorraine has produced one of the world's richest and most varied cuisines. It combines traditional French cooking with surprising and delicious ingredients. François Haeringer and his son, Jacques, have captured the flavor of Alsace in the hills outside Washington, D.C., home of L'Auberge Chez François, acclaimed "Bes Restaurant in Washington" for eight straight years by the readers of The Washingtonian Magazine. Roland F Mesnier, pastry chef at The White House writes "L'Auberge Chez François has been for many years my favorite restaurant and the favorite of many Washingtonians. What a treat to have Jacques Haeringer's wonderful recipes in such a beautiful book." He referred to The Chez François Cookbook by Jacques E. Haeringer. The restaurant opened April 20, 1976 and the youngest brother, Paul, joined the staff in 1979. "Paul's arrival completed my father's dream of a family run auberge," writes Jacques. The cuisine includes classics enjoyed by patrons for over 30 years, adaptation of regional American dishes, and current recipes.

What sounds like a side dish is a lovely light entree or special appetizer

Alsatian-Style Fresh Asparagus

PrepTime: 10 minutes
Cooking Time: 20-30 minutes
Servings Per Recipe: 4

1 In a saucepan, combine the water with the salt, bay leaves, and cloves and simmer for 15 minutes. Peel asparagus, cut off tough lower stems. Lay asparagus in a deep pan so that all tips are facing in the same direction. Cover asparagus with prepared seasoned water, bring to a boil and simmer 5-6 minutes. Drain at once on towels.

2 Preheat broiler. Pound veal to an even thickness (1/4-inch) with flat side of a meat cleaver (or kitchen mallet). Season meat with salt and pepper, and dredge in flour, shaking off the excess.

3 In a large sauté pan, combine 2 tablespoons of the butter and 1 tablespoon oil over high flame until butter begins to brown. Add veal and sauté quickly on both sides until lightly browned (1-2 minutes). Remove veal and keep warm. Add slices of ham and lightly sauté (about 20 seconds on each side).

4 Place a slice of veal and a slice of ham side by side on warm dinner plates. Arrange asparagus on top of meat and sprinkle with vinegar and capers. Top with grated cheese. Place prepared plates under broiler to brown the cheese.

5 Brown remaining butter. Remove plates from broiler and pour browned butter over asparagus. Garnish each plate with two quarters of hard-boiled egg and a sprig of fresh parsley. Serve immediately.

Use your favorite grated cheese in place of the Gruyère - keep in mind, some cheeses have a higher salt content than others.

2 quarts water

2 tablespoons salt

Bay leaves

Cloves

2 lb fresh jumbo asparagus

4 veal scallopini (cut from top round)

Salt and freshly ground black pepper

All-purpose flour

1 stick butter

1 tablespoon vegetable oil

4 slices dry cured ham

1 tablespoon red wine vinegar

2 teaspoons capers

8 tablespoons grated Gruyère cheese

2 hard-boiled eggs

4 sprigs parsley

Additional Equipment:

Kitchen mallet (optional)

A Taste Of Orlando

Jamison lamb and lobster in a roasted pumpkin with beurre blanc sauce

**Grand Floridian Resort & Spa,
Lake Buena Vista, FL (407)824-1089**

Victoria & Albert's Restaurant is an award-winning restaurant featuring two world class menus.

Chef Scott Hunnel tailors each course to perfection, from the luxury ingredients through preparation and plate design, to its presentation. His creations are truly something to behold.

An expertly appointed wine list assures your choice of the perfect wine to accompany your meal.

"Chefs to Keep Your Eye On" - Esquire

"Rising Star of American Cuisine" - Wine Spectator

"Top Ten in U.S.A." - Zagat Guide

"Top Ten Tables to Dine At" - Robb Report

Roasted Lamb and Lobster with Beurre Blanc

PrepTime: 360 minutes
Cooking Time: 60 minutes
Servings Per Recipe: 6

1 **Veal Stock:** Place the bones in a roasting pan in a hot oven at 375° F and brown them well. This will take 1 to 2 hours. Remove bones from pan and place in a stock pot. Cover with water and ice and bring to a simmer. Drain and reserve the fat in the roasting pan. Deglaze the pan with red wine and add to stock pot. Toss the onions, carrots, and celery with some of the reserved fat and brown well in the oven.

2 Add the browned vegetables, the tomato product, garlic, leek and herbs to the stock pot. Continue to simmer for a total cooking time of 4 hours, skimming the surface as necessary. Add water as needed to keep bones covered.

3 Strain stock through a chinois (fine mesh strainer) lined with several layers of cheese cloth. Cool the stock in a cold water bath and refrigerate overnight. The next day, skim all the remaining fat off the top of the stock. Place the stock back into a pot and reduce by 1/2 its original volume by simmering. This will take 1 to 2 hours. Skim the stock while reducing.

4 **Beurre Blanc:** In a sauce pot, reduce white wine and shallots until 1 tablespoon is left; add cream, cook down by half the volume (approximately 10 minutes) over medium heat. Remove from heat source and slowly whisk in butter. Season with salt and pepper.

5 **Vegetables:** Preheat oven to 400° F. Place 1 teaspoon each brown sugar and butter and a pinch of allspice into each pumpkin. Roast in oven for 30 minutes.

6 In a small pot of simmering water (2 cups water), add 2 tablespoons butter and 1 pinch of salt and pepper. Cook all vegetables in simmering water for approximately 3 minutes.

7 **Lamb and Lobster:** In a large pot of water, enough to submerge the lobsters, place lobsters into boiling water. Cook for 10 minutes. Pull out, de-shell lobster and keep warm.

8 Season lamb with salt and pepper, grill to desired temperature. Slice to create 3 bone racks.

9 **Putting it Together:** Place pumpkin on plate. Stuff with desired mashed potatoes (using a pastry bag). Place lobster inside and arrange vegetables in pumpkin (as shown in photo). Place lamb and claw on plate; drizzle or pour sauce on plate. Add final touches with the fresh herbs. Repeat with remaining pumpkins.

The veal stock is generally made the day before. Additional information: 1) Browning bones, the darker you can get them, without burning - the darker the final au jus. 2) Covering the roasted bones in ice water helps release the gelatin and yields a more flavorful au jus.

For the Veal Stock:
10-12 pounds lamb bones (cut into 3-4-inch pieces - butcher will cut for you)
10-12 quarts ice cold water
1 bottle Burgundy wine
1 lb onions, peeled and chopped
1 cup carrots, peeled and chopped
1 cup celery, chopped
1 lb tomatoes (or tomato puree)
2 cloves garlic, peeled and chopped
1 leek (white part only), sliced
6-8 parsley sprigs
1/4 teaspoon thyme
1 bay leaf

For the Beurre Blanc:
1 cup white wine
2 teaspoons shallots, peeled and chopped
1 cup heavy cream
1 cup butter, cubed
1 teaspoon salt
1/4 teaspoon pepper

For the Vegetables:
6 mini pumpkins, tops removed and cavity cleaned
6 teaspoons brown sugar
1/2 lb butter (divided)
6 pinches allspice
Pinch of salt and pepper (or to taste)
1 mini green zucchini
3 baby carrots
18 English peas
18 asparagus, peeled
18 yellow wax beans
6 chives

For the Lamb and Lobster:
3 live Maine lobsters (2 1/2-lbs each)
3 lamb racks, cleaned and frenched (have butcher clean)
Salt and pepper (to taste)
6 fresh basil leaves
1 cup lamb jus
Mashed potatoes (Yukon Gold or sweet potatoes), prepared

A Taste Of Salt Lake City

Crisp potato baskets filled with salad & red snapper-drizzled with a luscious vinaigrette

ITALIAN
Restaurant & Cafe
Grappa

151 Main St., Park City, UT
(435)645-0636

Located in a charming 100-year-old historic building reminiscent of a rustic Tuscan farmhouse, Grappa sits on a hillside at the top of Main Street in Salt Lake City

The food at Grappa is unequaled in quality, freshness and attention to detail. The wood-burning ovens, grills and rotisseries impart the special flavors of the South of France and all the regions of Italy.

Grappa is one of a select group that received the prestigious DiRoNA (Distinguished Restaurants of North America) award. Join Grappa for your favorite beverage, after-dinner desserts, pastries and delicacies, or sample their more elaborate Italian creations.

Seared Garlic Scaled Red Snapper

PrepTime: 45 minutes

Cooking Time: 60 minutes

Servings Per Recipe: 4

1 **Vinaigrette:** Coarsely chop tomatoes; combine them in a saucepan with tomato paste, olive oil, rosemary leaves, and garlic. Simmer over low heat for 20 minutes until olive oil has picked up the bright red-orange color from the tomatoes. Place this mixture in the blender or a food processor; blend together well and strain, reserving the "tomato oil." When cool, slowly add tomato oil to the vinegar while blending at medium speed. When mixed, add wild flower petals; season to taste with salt and pepper.

2 **Potato Basket:** In a deep pot, heat 4 cups of oil; while waiting for the oil to heat to 375° F, use a mandolin to cut one half of the first potato into long gaufrettes. Make only one basket at a time to avoid oxidation (discoloration) of potatoes. Do not put cut potatoes in water, as this will rinse away the starch that holds the basket together. Cut gaufrettes into small rectangles that match the height of your ring mold. After lightly oiling and dusting the mold with flour, place the potato strips around the mold. Hold them in place with a band of foil. Deep fry the basket until golden brown (about 3-5 minutes). Remove and let cool. With a tip of a paring knife gently remove the basket from the ring. Place on paper towels and reserve. Repeat these steps for remaining 3 baskets.

3 **Salad:** Clean and trim greens. Lightly blanch snow peas, baby carrots, and asparagus spears (to draw out color and improve the texture). Split carrots lengthwise, leaving tops on. Place prepared salad mix on a baking sheet lined with paper towels. Reserve in the refrigerator.

4 **Red Snapper:** Thinly slice garlic cloves on the mandolin (to make fish scales) and reserve. Lightly dust filets in flour and lay them in a skillet preheated with the olive oil. Sear both sides until medium rare (about 2-3 minutes). Remove fish but leave skillet on low flame. Drain fish well, blot excess oil with paper towels.

5 Lightly brush egg wash over filets and layer garlic scales onto the fish. When the scales are in place, cut four small pieces of foil, and place over the top of each fish. With the palm of your hand holding the foil against the scales, flip the filet, scale side down and place back into the hot seared pan. Turn up the heat to roast the garlic through the foil. This will take about 2 minutes.

6 **Putting it Together:** Arrange salads in potato baskets and place snapper on the plates. Drizzle the vinaigrette onto the plate and salad. Arrange garnishes and serve.

For the Vinaigrette:

6 Roma tomatoes

4 oz tomato paste

1/2 cup extra virgin olive oil

1 sprig rosemary (leaves only)

2 cloves garlic, peeled

3/8 cup red wine vinegar

2 oz (by volume) wild flower petals

Salt and pepper (to taste)

For the Potato Basket:

4 cups corn oil

2 large russet potatoes, washed

For the Salad:

12 oz assorted lettuces

12 snow peas

4 baby carrots (with tops)

8 asparagus spears

For the Red Snapper:

16 cloves fresh garlic (uniform in size), peeled and sliced using mandolin

2 (8-ounce) filets of red snapper (boned and skinned)

Flour (for dusting)

3/8 cup olive oil

1 egg, well beaten

Salt and pepper (to taste)

Garnish:

Assorted wild flowers

Chervil

Chives

Baby cherry tomatoes

Special Equipment:

12 1/2-inch ring mold

Mandolin (a manually operated slicer with adjustable blades), optional

A Taste Of Kansas City

Lamb Chops with Strada & Nicoise Olive Truffle Vinaigrette

Cafe Allegro

1815 W. 39th St., Kansas City, MO (816)561-366

Cafe Allegro has a long-standing award list in many categories from renowned food and wine critics. This chic bistro is considered Kansas City's most fashionable dining establishment for over a decade. Known for a casual, elegant atmosphere and intimate dining, Cafe Allego offers a very imaginative contemporary menu that transcends any one cuisine. It incorporates a variety of unique preparation methods and flavors. Stephen Cole's signature style of cooking has received national acclaim. The staff at Cafe Allegro will see to it that your dining experience is also nothing less than "award winning." For the dining experience that is truly exceptional in all aspects, Cafe Allegro is the choice of the most respected restaurant critics.

"Kansas City's Favorite Restaurant, Best Food, Best Service-1991, 1993, 1995, 1997" - Zagat Restaurant Survey

DiRoNa Award-1992, 1993, 1994, 1995, 1996, 1997, 1998

Grilled Rack of Lamb with Vegetable Strada

PrepTime: 60 minutes
Cooking Time: 25 minutes
Servings Per Recipe: 12

1 **Lamb:** In a mixing bowl, combine herbs, black pepper, garlic, and olive oil. Rub marinade all over each trimmed rack and set aside for grilling. When ready to grill (time it with your strada) - place marinated racks over prepared grill and cook to desired doneness.

2 **Vegetable Strada:** Dry out rounds of bread (set out overnight or baked in a 200° F oven for 1 hour). Set aside for assembly. In a 4-quart stainless steel sauce pot, heat 2 tablespoons olive oil. Add onions and cook over medium heat until translucent. Add garlic; stir and cook until aromatic (do not brown garlic). Add pear tomatoes and cook over low heat for 1 hour. Add sugar and oregano; season with salt and pepper, to taste. In a blender or food processor, puree sauce and set aside to cool. In a heated skillet with olive oil, brown the crimini mushrooms, then toss with garlic tomato sauce, and set aside to cool. In a heated skillet with olive oil, cook the diced peppers, zucchini, and eggplant until soft (5 minutes) and set aside to cool. Make custard by combining eggs, milk, and nutmeg. Assemble strada in 12 (8-ounce) ramekins (spray ramekins with non-stick cooking spray) - in the following order: 1 tablespoon tomato sauce, bread round, criminis, Asiago, bread round, 1 tablespoon tomato sauce, zucchini, peppers, eggplant, Asiago, spinach, bread round, 1 tablespoon tomato sauce, crumble of blue cheese; fill ramekin with custard. Bake in 400° F oven for 15-20 minutes. Flip out of ramekins onto serving plate.

3 **Vinaigrette:** In a nonreactive mixing bowl, combine vinegar, shallots, oregano, and garlic; slowly whisk in oils, then Nicoise olives.

4 **Putting it Together:** Rough chop radicchio and friseé. In a bowl, toss salad greens with vinaigrette. Arrange salad around strada on plate, then lean chops of grilled lamb against strada. Garnish with rosemary sprig or oregano.

Truffle oil and truffle vinegar can be purchased at specialty food shops.

For the Lamb Marinade:
12 racks of domestic lamb (4 chops each), frenched and trimmed
1/2 cup Italian parsley, minced
1/4 cup sage, minced
1/4 cup oregano, minced
1/4 cup thyme leaves
1/2 cup garlic, peeled and minced
1/4 cup freshly cracked black pepper
1/2 cup olive oil

For the Vegetable Strada:
36 (4 x 1/4-inch) rounds of French Farm Bread
Olive oil
1 onion, peeled and chopped
1/3 cup garlic, peeled and minced
6 cups pear tomatoes, in juice
2 tablespoons sugar
2 tablespoons oregano, minced
1 lb crimini mushrooms, thinly sliced
4-6 Anaheim peppers, seeds removed and cut into small dice
2 medium zucchini, seeds removed and cut into small dice
1 medium eggplant, seeds removed, and cut into small dice
Non-stick cooking spray
8 eggs
4 cups milk
1 teaspoon nutmeg
1 cup Asiago cheese, freshly grated
1 cup spinach, sautéed with 1 teaspoon garlic and drained
1 cup Maytag blue cheese

For the Nicoise Olive Truffle Vinaigrette:
1 cup extra virgin olive oil
1/4 cup white truffle oil
1/2 cup black truffle vinegar
2 tablespoons shallots, peeled and minced
2 tablespoons oregano, minced
1 tablespoon garlic, peeled and minced
Freshly cracked black pepper and salt (to taste)
1 head radicchio
2 heads frisée (a variety of endive)

For the Garnish:
Rosemary or oregano sprigs

Additional Equipment:
12 (8-ounce) ramekins

Pano's & Paul's

1232 W. Paces Ferry Rd., Atlanta, GA
(404)261-3662

Award-winning Pano's & Paul's is rated one of the top restaurants in the country for service. Open since 1979, Pano's & Paul's continues to provide a familiar yet exotic dinner menu, superior food presentation, a thoroughly experienced staff and a warm, plush interior.

They are not only renowned for the way they pamper their guests with unflappable European-style care in lavishly chic settings, but for their innovative yet comforting food prepared by highly trained chefs.

Pano's & Paul's American/Continental cuisine is enticing. According to Atlanta Magazine's food critic Christiane Lauterbach, "Pano's & Paul's is an institution, an Atlanta tradition. But far from dozing in the smugness of its success, the restaurant shows great vitality."

The restaurant is the flagship of the Buckhead Life Restaurant Group, which also operates 103 West, Buckhead Diner, Chops, Pricci, Veni Vidi Vici, and Atlanta Fish Market restaurant to name a few.

"4 Stars" - Mobil

"AAA Five Diamond Award"

For that very special dinner for two - this lobster and herbed risotto is simply perfect

Roasted Maine Lobster over Lemon Herb Risotto

PrepTime: 10 minutes
Cooking Time: 25 minutes
Servings Per Recipe: 2

1 **Lobster:** In a large stockpot, blanch lobster for 4 minutes. When cool enough to handle, twist off tail and cut in half; discard the intestine. Carefully crack the claw shells without breaking them up; remove meat from shell and set aside. Preheat oven and roasting pan to 400° F.

2 **Port Wine Sauce:** In a saucepan, reduce port wine and Burgundy until syrupy in consistency. Remove from heat and slowly whisk in butter; set aside.

3 **Risotto:** In a small pot, heat stock. In a medium saucepan, cook shallots in butter until transparent. Add rice, stirring until well coated, shiny and translucent. Turn up heat; add the wine. Cook over high heat until the wine evaporates. Turn the heat down, to simmer the rice. Slowly add hot stock until all the broth is absorbed in the rice. Turn off heat. Stir in cheese; season with salt and pepper to taste. Finish with lemon zest and herbs.

4 **Putting it Together:** Rub lobster tails and claws(meat) with olive oil and place on roasting pan. Roast for 5-6 minutes in preheated oven.

5 On a platter or plate, arrange lobster on top of risotto and garnish with some of the herbs and lemon zest. Finish the dish with the port wine reduction.

For the Lobster:

1 (2-pound) Maine lobster

2 tablespoons extra virgin olive oil

For the Port Wine Sauce:

1 cup port wine

2 cups Burgundy wine

8 tablespoons butter (salted)

For the Risotto:

1 cup stock (lobster or vegetable)

1 shallot, peeled and finely chopped

1 tablespoon butter

1/4 cup arborio rice

1/8 cup dry white wine

1 tablespoon Parmigiano-Reggiano cheese (or good Parmesan)

Salt and pepper (to taste)

Zest of 1 lemon

1 tablespoon parsley, chopped

2 tablespoons thyme leaves

A Taste Of New Jersey

Chicken in a rich creamy sauce with asparagus and shiitake mushrooms - a special entree

The Manor

111 Prospect Ave., West Orange, NJ
(973)731-2360

When Harry Knowles opened The Manor in the hills of West Orange on New Year's Eve 1956, he could not have known then that his dream would culminate in an establishment of which The New York Times said, "It is as close as one can get to perfection" and, more recently, "A class act ... almost too perfect to be true."

It has been a long and rewarding labor of love for Harry, Doris, Wade and Kurt Knowles. They have taken the original three rooms of The Manor and created a New Jersey dining environment that captures the timeless essence of elegance and splendor.

Now a landmark, The Manor has consistently received many coveted awards, a true indication of its superior quality standards.

"Business Executives' Dining Award"

"Grand Award" - Wine Spectator

"Four Diamond Award" - AAA

"DiRoNA Award"

Chicken Fricassée with Risotto and Vegetables

PrepTime: 30 minutes
Cooking Time: 120 minutes
Servings Per Recipe: 4

1 **Sauce:** In a large soup pot, place carrots, onion, leek, and celery root. Top with chicken and white wine. Fill the pot with water until chickens are covered. Add bay leaves, star anise, coriander, white pepper, and juniper berries. Bring to a boil over medium-high heat. Lower heat and simmer for 45 minutes. After 20 minutes, remove chickens from stock pot, and debone the breasts. Remove breast meat; set aside, returning remaining chicken to pot. When chicken is fully cooked, remove from the pot. Carefully remove all the bones and discard. Cut all of the chicken meat into small pieces and set aside.

2 Strain the broth. In a small pot, heat 2 cups of broth over medium-high heat; bring to a simmer and reduce by half. Add heavy cream and continue to reduce for 3 minutes. Mix a little cornstarch with cold water. Whisk evenly into sauce (as needed), and set aside.

3 **Risotto:** In a casserole, sauté the finely chopped shallots in olive oil with bouquet garni (tied herbs). Add rice and stir until evenly coated with olive oil. Sauté rice only until translucent. Add white wine and stir continuously. Add broth slowly while stirring. The rice is done when it is tender but firm to the bite (al dente). Remove from heat, add cheese and butter while stirring. Season with salt and pepper, to taste.

4 **Vegetables:** Peel asparagus and cut off ends. In a large pot of boiling, salted water, blanch asparagus. Remove asparagus from boiling water and place in ice water for 1 minute (to stop the cooking process).

5 In a large sauté pan, heat 1 tablespoon of butter over medium high heat. Add mushrooms. Sauté until golden brown. Season with salt and pepper.

6 **Putting it Together:** To a Dutch oven or oven proof dish add chicken pieces, asparagus, mushrooms, and sauce. Heat sauce over medium high heat. Add orange juice, zest, and ginger. Season with salt and pepper, to taste. Whisk in remaining tablespoon of butter until melted and serve.

Many ingredients can be added to risotto to make interesting dishes - seafood, meat, vegetables or mushrooms.

For the Fricassée:
4 carrots, peeled and diced
3 large onions, peeled and diced
1 leek, peeled and diced
1 knob celery root, peeled and diced
2 whole free range chickens
2 cups dry white wine
Water (as needed)
4 bay leaves
1 star anise
1 tablespoon coriander seed
1 tablespoon whole white peppercorns
1 tablespoon juniper berries
2 cups heavy cream
Cornstarch (as needed)
Zest and juice of 1 orange
1 oz fresh ginger root, peeled, grated and squeezed through a cheesecloth (retain liquid)
Salt and pepper (to taste)

For the Risotto:
3 shallots, peeled and finely diced
3 tablespoons extra virgin olive oil
Bouquet garni: sprigs of thyme, rosemary and sage tied at stem ends or in a bundle
1/2 lb superfino rice (arborio or carnaroli)
2 cups dry white wine
1 1/4 cups chicken stock
3 oz Parmesan cheese
8 tablespoons butter
Salt and pepper (to taste)

For the Vegetables:
2 bundles asparagus (white preferably)
2 tablespoons butter (divided)
8 oz shiitake mushrooms, cleaned, stems removed and sliced evenly

A Taste Of San Diego

*Rare peppered tuna on basil oil with a
balsamic vinegar reduction and saffron risotto*

801 5th Ave., San Diego, CA (619)234-3467

*Since 1989, Fio's Cucina Italiana, the dining mecca of
downtown San Diego's exuberant Gaslamp Quarter
National Historic District, has been voted the county's
"Favorite Italian Restaurant" every year by diners and
food critics alike. The reason is simple: Fio's doesn't rest
on its laurels.*

*Its sophisticated dinner menu changes seasonally, so
guests can savor the freshest, most delightful and finest
cuisine available. Its homemade pastas, breads and
desserts are heavenly. Its pre-theater and special-occasion
menus and nightly dinner specials are the city's most
imaginative. Fio's stylish dining rooms, award-winning
wine collection, comfortable lounge with full bar,
delightful patio dining and gracious service are
unexcelled.*

Costolette di Tonno al Ventura

PrepTime: 15 minutes
Cooking Time: 20 minutes
Servings Per Recipe: 4

1 **Basil Oil: Needs to be refrigerated for 2 days prior to use.** In a large pot, blanch the herbs in boiling, salted water. Remove and shock in cold water; drain. Rough chop blanched herbs, squeeze out excess water place in blender with enough oil to cover. Puree well, slowly adding remaining oil. Pour into container and refrigerate for 2 days. Strain through a chinois (fine mesh strainer) before use.

2 **Seared Peppered Ahi:** Press ahi steaks with peppercorns. In a very hot sauté pan with peanut oil, sear ahi steaks for 10 seconds. Turn carefully and sear for 10 seconds. Remove from pan and slice.

3 **Balsamic Glaze:** In a small saucepan over medium heat, slowly reduce balsamic vinegar until syrup consistency.

4 **Saffron Risotto:** In a heavy, nonreactive skillet, heat olive oil and sauté onion and shallots until golden. Add rice and stir, to coat with oil; add wine and stir well. To the hot stock, add 1 teaspoon saffron. Add 1/2 cup of hot stock and salt to the skillet; cook stirring constantly, until all liquid has been absorbed. Continue to add hot stock in small batches (just enough to completely moisten rice) and cook until each successive batch has been absorbed, stirring constantly until rice mixture is creamy and al dente.

5 Remove from heat, whip in butter and half of the grated cheese. Season with salt and freshly ground pepper. Top each serving with additional grated cheese to taste; serve immediately.

6 **Putting it Together:** When ready to serve, place some basil oil on plate, center the risotto and fan out tuna around the rice. Dot with the balsamic reduction in whatever pattern desired.

For the Basil Oil:

1 1/2 cups basil leaves

1/2 cup Italian parsley

1 1/2 cups blend oil

1/2 cup olive oil

For the Seared Peppered Ahi:

4 (7-ounce) ahi (number 1 grade)

1/2 cup crushed black peppercorns

1/4 cup peanut oil

For the Balsamic Glaze:

1/2 cup balsamic vinegar

For the Risotto Saffron:

3 tablespoons olive oil

1 cup onion, peeled and minced

2 tablespoons shallots, peeled and minced

2 cups arborio or carnaroli rice

1/2 cup dry white wine

1 teaspoon saffron

6 cups hot chicken stock (Homemade or prepared)

1/2 teaspoon salt (or to taste)

2 tablespoons butter, cut into small pieces

1/2 cup freshly grated Parmigiano-Reggiano cheese

Freshly ground pepper (to taste)

Marinated grilled tuna with a Szechuan peppercorn sauce

2000 Sidney St., St. Louis, MO
(314)771-5777

Sidney Street Café is an indoor courtyard café with polished hardwood floors, exposed bricks, street lamps and a wonderful old-fashioned bar. Housed in a 100-year-old building, this Benton Park neighborhood restaurant has been completely renovated in keeping with its turn-of-the-century roots.

Since 1985, Sidney Street Café has been serving new American and Continental dishes, including fresh seafood, chicken, pastas and hand-cut steaks, with an emphasis on herbs, sauces and presentation.

A perfect meal at Sidney's might start with their famed Bleu Cheese Tart, or the big Stuffed Mushrooms in a light cheese sauce, followed by Lamb Chops in an oriental glaze or perfectly cooked pasta in a seafood sauce thick with mussels, shrimp and crab meat. Delicious.

A lovely garden room filled with beautiful tiles, plants and skylights is perfect for private parties.

Seared Tuna with Szechuan Sauce

PrepTime: 60 + minutes
Cooking Time: 10 + minutes
Servings Per Recipe: 4

1 **Tuna:** In a large bowl, combine teriyaki sauce, olive oil, garlic, cracked pepper, pepper flakes, chili sauce, oyster sauce, green onions, cilantro, lime juice, and ginger. Mix thoroughly. Marinate tuna for 1 hour before cooking (up to 24 hours - refrigerated).

2 In a large sauté pan or on a flat grill over high heat, sear tuna on each side to desired doneness.

3 **Szechuan Tuna Sauce:** In a large sauce pan, combine sherry, chili sauce, wasabi paste, sesame oil, orange zest, teriyaki sauce, peppercorns, and ginger. Bring to boil until wine is reduced. Add cream and bring to boil; reduce by half.

4 **Putting it Together:** On serving plate, place pickled ginger, seared tuna filet, then top with Szechuan Tuna Sauce and garnish with slivered carrots and green onions.

For the Tuna:
4 tuna filets (3-inches thick)
1/4 cup teriyaki sauce
1/2 cup olive oil
1 tablespoon garlic, peeled and crushed
1 tablespoon cracked pepper
1 tablespoon red pepper flakes
1 tablespoon Chinese chili sauce
2 tablespoons oyster sauce
1 tablespoon green onions, finely chopped
1 tablespoon cilantro, chopped
1/4 cup lime juice
1 tablespoon fresh ginger, peeled and minced

For the Szechuan Tuna Sauce:
1/4 cup sherry
1 teaspoon Chinese chili sauce
1/2 teaspoon wasabi paste
1 teaspoon sesame oil
1 teaspoon orange zest
1/4 cup teriyaki sauce
1 teaspoon Szechuan peppercorns
1 teaspoon pickled ginger, finely chopped
1/2 cup cream

For the Garnish:
Slivered carrots
Slivered green onions
Pickled ginger

A Taste Of Minneapolis

Goodfellow's
An American Restaurant

40 So. 7th St., Minneapolis, MN (612)332-4800

Located in the heart of downtown Minneapolis, Goodfellow's serves award-winning American regional cuisine in an elegant and historic Art Deco environment. Goodfellow's wine list has also brought home its share of awards.

In addition to its wonderful cuisine, excellent wine list and lovely dining room, Goodfellow's lounge is a great place to meet after work or before the show. Private dining is available for groups from eight to 80.

"DiRoNA Award"

"Four Diamond" - AAA

"Award of Excellence" Wine Spectator

Nation's Restaurant News Hall of Fame

Tuna and venison ravioli with roasted mushrooms & Cabernet chipotle demi-glace

Seared Ahi Tuna with Venison Ravioli

PrepTime: 120 minutes
Cooking Time: 8-10 minutes
Servings Per Recipe: 6

1 **Ravioli:** Place egg and water in bowl and whisk in salt. Add semolina and flour and mix in mixer with paddle attachment, or by hand. Roll out dough using a pasta machine, as thin as possible. Egg wash pasta dough. Place venison in middle of the dough and top with onion and garlic. Fold the dough over and press the dough down with fingers. Cut ravioli into 2-inch size shapes. Push out air and reserve in semolina dust.

2 **Cabernet Sauce:** Place wine, ginger, and chipotle in a saucepan, and cook until it reduces down by one-third. Add demi-glace and reduce to consistency of coating the back of a spoon; strain and reserve sauce.

3 **Roasted Shiitake:** Coat mushroom caps with canola oil and place on baking sheet. Roast in a 400° F oven until wilted (brown, not crisp). When cooked, julienne, and reserve.

4 **When Ready to Serve:** Bring a large pot of salted water to a boil - place ravioli in pot and boil for 15 seconds (making sure dough is al dente). Remove from water and rinse.

5 **Ahi Tuna:** In a skillet, add peanut oil and heat to almost smoking. Add tuna and sear on both sides - cook to desired doneness. (Chef recommends keeping it rare if sushi grade.)

6 **Putting it Together:** On a serving plate, pour some of the Cabernet sauce, top with seared tuna and garnish with shiitake mushrooms and ravioli.

For the Ravioli:

1 egg

1 2/3 tablespoon water (more as needed)

1 teaspoon salt

1 cup semolina

1/2 cup all purpose flour

1 egg, whipped (egg wash)

For the Venison Ravioli Filling:

1 1/2 cups braised venison

1/2 sweet onion, julienned and sautéed

36 cloves of roasted garlic, peeled and sliced

For the Cabernet Sauce:

1 1/2 cups Cabernet wine

1/4 cup fresh ginger, peeled and grated

1 chipotle chile

1/2 cup veal demi-glace

For the Roasted Shiitake:

12 oz shiitake mushrooms, cleaned and stems removed

2 tablespoons canola oil

For the Ahi Tuna:

1 teaspoon peanut oil

6 (3 oz each) center cut ahi tuna

Game at its finest, rubbed with coriander and pepper— topped with The Riviera Steak Sauce

THE RIVIERA

7709 Inwood Rd., Dallas, TX
(214)351-0094

Since opening its beautiful curtained French doors in 1984, The Riviera has created the perfect romantic setting for an unforgettable dining experience.

With its refined atmosphere and sophisticated menu inspired by the flavors and ingredients of Northern Italy and Southern France, The Riviera evokes the atmosphere of the elegant country inns of Provence.

While keeping an eye on the kitchen at The Riviera, Executive Chef David Holben and Proprietor Franco Bertolasi have opened the Mediterraneo, Mediterraneo at the Quadrangle and Toscana restaurants.

"Top Table and Best Food Award" - Gourmet Magazine

Inductee into the "Nation's Restaurant News" Hall of Fame

Consistently high ratings in the Zagat Guide

"Mumm's Cuvee Napa Award" Condè Nast Traveler Magazine

Top 10 New Chefs of America - Food & Wine Magazine

Cervena Venison and Tomato-Eggplant Gratin

PrepTime: 180 + minutes
Cooking Time: 20 minutes
Servings Per Recipe: 6

1 **Steak Sauce:** In a large non-reactive sauce pan, saute the onions, shallots, anchovy, and minced garlic in olive oil. Add the chopped tomato and the tomato paste, and continue to cook for 2 minutes. Place the rest of the ingredients, except for the soy sauce, salt and pepper, in the sauce pan and reduce until a sauce consistency. Remember to skim the sauce frequently.

2 Transfer sauce to a blender or food processor, and pulse on and off 4-6 times. Season with soy sauce, salt and pepper.

3 **Coriander Rub:** Puree all of the ingredients for the Coriander Rub in a food processor until ingredients are incorporated. Add extra oil if mixture seems to dry.

4 **Venison:** Coat all sides of the venison lightly with the rub. Refrigerate the venison for 3-4 hours.

5 In a large skillet over high heat, sear the venison in a small amount of olive oil. Place venison in a 350° F oven for 5-8 minutes or until medium-rare. Let stand 5 minutes before serving.

6 **Gratin:** In a large skillet, sauté the onion in olive oil; add a pinch of salt and cook until transparent.

7 Brush both sides of the tomatoes and eggplant with olive oil, and sprinkle with the rosemary and thyme; season with salt and pepper. Grill the eggplant on both sides until tender (2-3 minutes), and 1-2 minutes for the tomatoes.

8 On a lightly oiled baking sheet, place 3 slices of eggplant slightly overlapping to form a circle. Place 2 tablespoons of cooked onions on top and spread out evenly. Arrange tomatoes, on top (using both colors). Repeat 5 times with remaining ingredients. Keep in oven at 350° F until warm.

9 **Putting it Together:** Place a stack of vegetable gratin in center of plate, slice the venison 3/8 inch thick and fan 4-5 slices on top. Drizzle with sauce.

Garnish with 12 stalks of blanched asparagus sliced on a bias 1/2-inch long, diced yellow and red bell peppers and salt and pepper to taste.

For the Steak Sauce:
3 tablespoons onion, chopped
1/2 cup shallots
1 tablespoon anchovy, chopped
2 teaspoons garlic, minced
2 tablespoons olive oil
3/4 cup tomatoes, chopped
1/4 cup tomato paste
1 teaspoon chile flakes
1/4 cup + 1 tablespoon Worcestershire Sauce
1 cup molasses
2 tablespoons corn syrup
1/2 cup brandy
1/4 cup red wine vinegar
1/4 cup balsamic vinegar
1 cup veal glaze
2 tablespoons tamarind paste
1 quart demi-glace
Soy sauce (to taste)
Salt and pepper (to taste)

For the Coriander Rub:
3/4 cup cracked black pepper
1 cup garlic cloves
1 cup brown sugar
2 tablespoons kosher salt
1/2 cup thyme, chopped
1/4 cup coriander, toasted and ground fine
3/4 cup sage, chopped
1/4 cup olive oil

For the Venison:
2 1/2 lb Cervena Denver leg or Cervena loin, trimmed evenly

For the Gratin:
2 medium onions, thinly sliced
1/4 cup olive oil
Pinch salt
18 slices red tomatoes, 3/8 inch thick
18 slices yellow tomatoes, 3/8 inch thick
18 slices eggplant, 3/8 inch thick
3 tablespoons fresh rosemary, chopped
3 tablespoons fresh thyme, chopped

A Taste Of Phoenix

Lamb served on green bean and mushroom ragout with fingerling potatoes

LONs
at the hermosa

**5532 N. Palo Cristi Rd., Paradise Valley, AZ
(602)955-7878**

LON's at the hermosa is located at the historic Hermosa Inn, a building done in the traditional hacienda-style of architecture. LON's embraces all that is Southwest, with its decor of rustic Southwestern furnishings and artifacts.

LON's also embraces contemporary American dining featuring the award-winning American Cuisine of Executive Chef Patrick Poblete.

Chef Poblete creates specialty menu items that reflect each season's bounty. To be sure of the freshest ingredients, he uses fresh produce from a 10,000-square-foot garden located on the property.

Chef Poblete's New Zealand Rack of Lamb, is accompanied by a ragout of mushrooms, corn, red bell peppers, green beans and fingerling potatoes.

"One of the top four restaurants in Phoenix" - USA Today

"Hottest New Restaurant" - National Food & Wine Magazine

"Best Brunch" - Phoenix Magazine

New Zealand Rack of Lamb

PrepTime: 30 minutes

Cooking Time: 20-40 minutes

Servings Per Recipe: 4

1 Preheat oven to 350° F. In a bowl, toss fingerling potatoes in olive oil, salt and pepper. Place coated potatoes in a roasting pan, bake for 20-30 minutes, or until done. Set potatoes aside; keep warm.

2 Rub olive paste on lamb and season with salt and pepper. In preheated sauté pan, sear lamb and place in a preheated 350° F oven for 20-40 minutes (or cook to desired doneness).

3 In preheated sauté pan, add olive oil and sauté green beans and button mushrooms; add Portabella mushrooms. Stir vegetables and allow to cook 2-3 minutes. Add corn and red peppers; cook vegetables an additional 4-6 minutes. Season with salt and pepper, to taste.

4 **Putting it Together:** Place a generous tablespoon of vegetables in center of serving plate; top with 4-5 pieces (3 ounces per serving) of fingerling potatoes. Slice lamb rack in half and place one half on its side and other half standing up. Place pea shoot sprouts in center between two lamb portions.

5 Place lamb sauce (of your choice) or condiment (chutney) around the base, and serve.

Prepared Lamb Sauce, Chutney and Fruit Condiments are available at specialty food shops.

12 oz fingerling potatoes

Olive Oil

Salt and pepper (to taste)

1/2 cup olive paste

11-12 oz New Zealand rack of lamb

1/2 cup green beans, trimmed and cut on bias (1-inch)

1/2 cup button mushrooms, cleaned and sliced

4 oz Portabella mushrooms, cleaned and sliced

1 corn on the cob, kernels removed

1 red bell pepper, seeded, deveined and cut to medium dice

1/4 cup pea shoot sprouts

Lamb sauce or condiment of choice

A Taste New Orleans

Mr. B's BBQ shrimp makes a great appetizer or a terrific light entree

201 Royal St., New Orleans, LA (504)523-2078

In the heart of the French Quarter, Mr. B's Bistro is a major player in the ongoing process of redefining New Orleans cooking. Louisiana is a melting pot of cultures French, Spanish, Italian, African American, Indian and Caribbean. The culinary result is Creole Cuisine and is always evolving towards new and better taste sensations. In that spirit, Mr. B's adapts and incorporates local and regional ingredients into innovative Creole creations.

Today, Cindy Brennan, owner and operator, is proud to offer her own special take on regional Creole cuisine, strong in its flavorful ties both to New Orleans and South Louisiana.

Mr. B's embraces the challenge to serve simple and honest bistro-style food for an all-occasion business lunch, a festive jazz brunch or dinner accompanied by live piano music. Mr. B's Bistro strives to deliver a great experience.

"Best Business Lunch" - Food & Wine Magazine 1998

"Top for Business" - Gourmet Magazine 1998

Barbecued Shrimp

PrepTime: 15 minutes
Cooking Time: 10 minutes
Servings Per Recipe: 2

1 **Creole Seasoning:** In a mixing bowl add salt, garlic, black pepper, cayenne, thyme, oregano, paprika and onion. Store in an airtight container.

2 **Shrimp:** Heat a sauté pan over high heat. Put shrimp, Worcestershire, both black peppers, Creole seasoning and garlic into pan; add 3 tablespoons water to pan. Squeeze lemon half into pan; cook until shrimp are cooked half way and liquid is reduced (about 4 minutes).

3 Add butter, swirling pan gently to incorporate. Serve when shrimp are cooked through and sauce is proper consistency (about another 4 minutes).

4 **Putting it Together:** Place cooked shrimp in a bowl and pour sauce over. Garnish with hot French bread (for dipping).

Use extra Creole Seasoning on your favorite meats, fish and poultry. Will keep in an airtight container.

For the Creole Seasoning:

1 cup salt

4 tablespoons granulated garlic

4 tablespoons ground black pepper

1 teaspoon cayenne pepper

1 teaspoon thyme

1 teaspoon oregano

4 tablespoons paprika

1 tablespoon granulated onion

For the Shrimp:

8 large shrimp (with heads on)

1/4 cup Worcestershire Sauce

1 teaspoon fine black pepper

1 teaspoon cracked black pepper

1 teaspoon Creole Seasoning (see recipe)

1/2 teaspoon fresh garlic, peeled and chopped

1/2 fresh lemon

12 tablespoons cold unsalted butter (cut into 6 equal potions)

For the Garnish:

Hot French Bread

A Taste Of Central Valley

ERNA'S
ELDERBERRY
HOUSE

48688 Victoria Lane, Oakhurst, CA (209)683-680

Upholding the excellence of the European Grand Manor Houses, Chateau du Sureau, with its ten enchanting guest rooms, sits on nine wooded acres surrounded by beautiful hillside gardens and offers its guests a stay in the traditions of long ago.

A short stroll across the gardens leads to Erna's Elderberry House, where award-winning California-French Cuisine awaits in understated country elegance. Chef James Overbaugh's six-course prix-fixe menus change nightly based on the freshest ingredients available. His innovative food has received high ratings from the 1998 Zagat Guide. Popular cooking classes combined with wine seminars are held thrice a year, offering a dynamic, personal culinary getaway for those who wish to combine luxurious accommodations with the rewarding joy of cooking (and eating!).

The unconditional commitment to excellence has earned Chateau du Sureau the highest honor from Mobil Travel the Five Star Award. Both the hotel and restaurant have earned the Five Diamond Award from AAA. It is also a member of the prestigious Relais & Chateaux Group.

Hearty and seafood laden - make sure you have plenty of grilled French bread

Bouillabaisse de La Maison

PrepTime: 30 minutes
Cooking Time: 45 minutes
Servings Per Recipe: 6

1 In a large heavy pot, sauté onions, fennel and carrot in olive oil, until soft. Add roasted garlic and vermouth; reduce until alcohol is cooked off.

2 Add fish broth, coriander, fennel seeds, orange zest, parsley, thyme, bay leaf, and saffron. Simmer until flavors are infused. Add Pernod and lightly seasoned fish. Cook to halfway point, add tomatoes, potato cubes, and basil. Season with salt and pepper.

3 Serve bouillabaisse in warmed bowls with grilled French bread and garnish with reserved basil leaves.

1 small onion, peeled and thinly sliced

1 bulb fennel, thinly sliced

1 medium carrot, peeled and thinly sliced

2 tablespoons olive oil

1 bulb roasted garlic, with softened cloves removed and mashed (amount will depend on strength)

1 cup dry vermouth

5-6 cups fish stock

1/2 teaspoon toasted coriander seeds, lightly crushed

1/2 teaspoon fennel seeds, lightly crushed

Pinch of orange zest

Parsley

Sprig of thyme, chopped

2 bay leaves

Pinch of saffron

2 tablespoons Pernod (licorice-flavored)

1/2 pound rock shrimp

6 fanny bay oysters, shucked

1/4 pound salmon, cut into 2/3-inch pieces

2 medium tomatoes, peeled, seeded and diced

1 large russet potato, peeled, small cubed and blanched

8 stems of basil (reserve 6 leaves for garnish) chiffonade remaining

Salt and pepper (to taste)

French bread

Measurements & Equivalents

Teaspoon	Tablespoon	Cup	Fluid ounce
1	1/3	~	~
3	1	~	1/2
6	2	1/8	1
12	4	1/4	2
~	8	1/2	4
~	12	3/4	6
~	16	1	8

Note: These equivalents are approximations only.

Pinch or dash
Less than 1/8 teaspoon

2 Cups
1 pint or 16 fl oz

4 Quarts
1 gallon or 128 fl oz

4 Pecks
1 bushel

1 Stick of butter
8 tablespoons or 1/2 cup

1 Lemon
(depending on the size)
2-3 tablespoons juice or
1 tablespoon grated peel

4 Cups
1 quart or 32 fl oz

2 Gallons
8 quarts or 1 peck

1 Jigger
3 tablespoons
or 1 1/2 fl oz

4 Sticks of butter
1 lb or 2 cups

1 Slice of bread
1/2 cup bread crumbs

Fahrenheit Setting	Celsius Setting*	Gas Setting
300°F	150°C	Gas Mark 2
325°F	160°C	Gas Mark 3
350°F	180°C	Gas Mark 4
375°F	190°C	Gas Mark 5
400°F	200°C	Gas Mark 6
425°F	220°C	Gas Mark 7
450°F	230°C	Gas Mark 8
BROIL		GRILL

*As a good rule of thumb, increase the Celsius setting by 10-20° when cooking above 160° Celsius with an electric oven. For convection or forced-air ovens, lower the Celsius setting by 10° Celsius when cooking at all heat levels.

substitutions

To truly enjoy the flavors of the recipes, it is always best to have the specified ingredients; however, when caught in a pinch, here are some suggestions...

Sorrel or "Greens"
Use spinach (equal parts)

Fennel
Use celery (equal parts)

1 Cup Sugar
Use 7/8 cup honey

Sea Salt
(or any iodized salt product)
Use kosher salt (equal parts)

1 Clove Garlic
Use 1/8 teaspoon garlic powder or 1/8 teaspoon minced dried garlic or 1/2 teaspoon jarred garlic

1 Small Onion
Use 1 teaspoon onion powder or 1 tablespoon minced dried onion, rehydrated

1 Cup Tomato Sauce
Use 3 oz tomato paste plus 1/2 cup water

Sake or Rice Wine
Use dry sherry or dry vermouth (equal parts)

Fish Stock
Use equal parts clam juice and water

1 Tablespoon Fish Sauce
Use 2 teaspoons soy sauce with 2 mashed anchovies

Pancetta
Use cooked lean bacon (equal parts)

Pine Nuts
Use walnuts or almonds (equal parts)

Prosciutto
Use country ham (equal parts)

Fresh Chives
Use green onions, including the tops (equal parts)

Cocktail Sauce
Use ketchup with prepared horseradish and lemon juice (to taste)

For the Health Conscious	
Use...	**In Place of...**
Anchovies	salt for salad dressings
Carrots	sugar for sauces (equal parts)
Chicken Stock	oil or fat in cooking (equal parts)
1 Cup Plain Yogurt	1 cup sour cream
7/8 Cup Vegetable Oil	1/2 lb (2 sticks) butter
Lemon Juice	salt for seasoning soups and stocks

II

Wine Suggestions

Red Wine

Produced from black grapes; contact between the skins and the juice during the fermentation process develops the range of color from pink to deep red.

Rosé Wine

Produced from black grapes; grape skins are left in contact with the fermenting juice just long enough to achieve the desired color. Rosé can range in hue from barely peach to an intense pink.

White Wine

Produced from white grapes (and sometimes from red grapes) having little, or no, contact between the skins and the fermenting juice—keeping it pale in color.

Sparkling Wine
(effervescent)

A wine bottled with carbon dioxide; produced by either méthode champenoise or Charmat process.

Standard Pairings
Match the wine to the strongest flavor on your plate

Rich Full Bodied Reds	*Wild Game*	Côte-Rôtie, Syrah, Zinfandel
Full Bodied to Medium Bodied Reds	*Beef, Lamb, Duck, Pasta with Red Sauce*	Red Burgundy/Pinot Noir, Cabernet Sauvignon, Merlot, Chianti Classico
Medium Bodied to Light Bodied Reds	*Pork Products and Ground Meats*	Young Bordeaux, Valpolicella, Beaujolais Cru
Light Bodied Reds	*Veal and Chicken*	Alsatian/German Pinot Noir, Beaujolais, Dry Rosé
Full Bodied/Oak-Aged Whites	*Salmon, Lobster, and Crab*	White Burgundy, Pouilly-Fumé, White Rhône, Pinot Grigio, California Chardonnay
Medium Bodied Whites	*Fish*	Chablis, Pinot Blanc, Chenin Blanc, Soave
Medium to Light Bodied Whites	*Shrimp and Scallops (small crustaceans)*	Sauvignon Blanc, Dry Riesling, Gewürztraminer
Light Crisp Wines	*Oysters and Mussels*	German Riesling, Viognier
Dessert Wines		Muscat, Late-harvest Riesling, Sauternes

Split . . . . 6.3 U.S. ounces - 187 ml
Half bottle . . . . 12.7 U.S. ounces - 375 ml
Standard bottle . . . . 25.4 U.S. ounces - 750 ml

Liter . . . . 33.8 ounces - 1 liter
Magnum . . . . 50.7 U.S. ounces - 1 1/2 liters
Standard Glass Portion . . 5 U.S. Ounces - 140 grams

Herbs, Spices and Aromatics

Basil — Ranging in both color and pungency, basil is easy to use with recipes calling for tomatoes, eggs, poultry, lamb, veal, fish, pasta, beans, grains, mushrooms, nuts, zucchini, and cheese. Delicious in salads, rice dishes, stuffing and crepes, this leaf intensifies during the cooking process.

Cilantro — Often called Chinese or Mexican parsley, cilantro is frequently used in ethnic foods. Its distinctive flavor marries well with beans, grains, rice, vegetables (salsas and salads), meats, fish, shellfish and poultry.

Coriander — With its mild slightly orange spicy-sweet flavor, this spherical seed is commonly used whole as a pickling spice or ground in recipes containing meat, rice and vegetables. The flavorful leaves are named cilantro.

Curry Powder — Traditionally used in Indian and Caribbean cuisine, its spicy flavor marries well with beans, grains, rice, vegetables, meats, fish, shellfish, and poultry. Try in chicken and vegetable-based soups.

Elephant Garlic — Members of the onion family, these cloves are milder than regular garlic, and offer a nice addition to recipes that require subtle flavor.

Ginger — Pungent and aromatic, this brown-skinned root is terrific in marinades, salad dressings, stir-fry and sushi. Great added to teas, or candied and eaten as a sweet, and marries well with cinnamon, cloves, nutmeg, garlic and chives.

Marjoram — A member of the mint family and closely resembling mild oregano, marjoram compliments the flavors of meat (all types), roasted poultry, tomatoes, green vegetables, mushrooms and pasta.

Nutmeg — This strong, flavorful seed that comes from the nutmeg tree (a type of evergreen) is generally associated with sweets; however, adds a new dimension to cream sauces and soups.

When using fresh herbs is not possible, dried herbs may be used in their place.

*~A rough estimate ~
For every tablespoon
of Fresh, use
one teaspoon of Dried.*

Remember that less is more, so taste before adding more.

Oregano — Closely associated with wild marjoram, the distinctive and peppery flavor of oregano is commonly teamed up with thyme in a variety of recipes. Often found in Italian, Greek and Mexican cuisine, this herb often finds its way into recipes that call for tomatoes, meat sauces, beef, pork, veal and lamb.

Rosemary — The gray-green needle-shaped leaves from this branchy herb infuse the strong flavors of lemon and pine into grilled meats and fish, as well as roasted poultry.

Sage — A fragrant sub-shrub, this musty-flavored herb is often added to stuffing and savory dishes containing sausage, duck, pheasant, strong cheese and beans.

Shallots — A member of the onion family, their delicate flavor is perfect for sauces, salad dressings and marinades.

Tarragon — Common to France and Russia, its faintly anise-like flavor pairs well with vinegar for vinaigrette dressings, mayonnaise, eggs, fish and most vegetables.

Thyme — Having many species and flavors, the sprigs are often used in flavoring vinegar, meats, soups and chowders.

Turmeric — Often used in Asian and Indian cuisine, this yellow-orange slightly bitter member of the ginger family is used to give color to prepared sauces and mustard.

Glossary

Al Dente — Italian word for "to the tooth". Term used to describe pasta (also vegetables and rice) cooked to firm.

Arborio rice — Italian, short-grained rice, used in risotto. This mild white rice has a creamy consistency.

Blanching *(blanch)* — The process of immersing food for a brief time in boiling water, then plunging into cold water to stop the cooking process. Generally, blanching is used to help remove the peel of fruits and vegetables, to remove raw flavors or to quick-cook something prior to freezing.

Braising *(braise)* — The process of cooking meat (and sometimes vegetables) in hot fat, then placing in a covered pot with a small amount of liquid, and cooking over low heat. This process is generally used for tougher cuts of meat.

Butterfly — The technique of cutting boneless meat in a horizontal direction, without going all the way through, opening it like butterfly wings. This process is usually done by the butcher, but can easily be done by home cooks for stuffing roasts, chicken breasts, fish, or enlarging the surface of shrimp.

Caper — Unopened flower buds of a low-growing shrub Capparis spinosa, indigenous to Mediterranean areas. The green buds are pickled and used as flavorings or condiments.

Caramelize *(caramelization)* — The natural process of cooking foods that contain natural sugar (i.e., onions) to a melting point, until they turn golden brown.

Chinois *(China Cap)* — A kitchen tool — a fine mesh cone-shaped sieve with a handle or legs, often accompanied by a cone-shaped wooden plunger. It is perfect for fine purées (sauces and coulis) and straining stocks.

Chutney — A condiment or side dish made from fruits and vegetables and cooked with sugar, spices and vinegar — generally accompanying meat, fish or poultry. Chutney is often used with curries and ranges in texture, as well as hotness of flavor.

Clarified butter — The process of making butter clear by heating, separating and removing the milk solids (also referred to as drawn butter).

Coulis — A sauce made from a fine purée of fruits or vegetables. While used as a sauce, it makes a striking garnish.

Couscous — Native to North Africa, this grain-like pasta has become a trendy staple to fill in for potatoes or rice.

Deglaze — The process of first adding liquid to a pan that has been roasting or cooking for a period of time, and then stirring to dissolve all of the solids to liquid form. It is often used for sauces and as a base for stocks.

Demi-glace — Result of reducing brown sauce/brown stock by half — can be purchased at specialty food stores.

Dredge *(dredging)* — The process of coating a food with flour, finely ground crumbs or flakes (bread, cracker, cornmeal, corn flakes, etc.).

Food mill — A kitchen tool; a hand cranked sieve-like system with interchangeable disks, for the purpose of filtering and puréeing fruits and vegetables.

Garnish — To embellish or decorate a plate, platter or food with something edible. Also, a secondary food that adds flavor, texture and color to the focal ingredients.

Julienne — The process of cutting food into match stick shapes of equal size. This can be achieved by hand or with the use of a kitchen mandoline or slicer. Often used in salad, stir-fry and as a garnish.

Phyllo *(Filo)* — Paper-thin layered sheets of pastry dough — homemade or purchased (usually found in the freezer section of most groceries) and used in the preparation of desserts or savory foods. Once considered an ethnic food item, it is now mainstream.

Poaching — The process of cooking food slowly in heated liquid (i.e., wine, milk, water) below the boiling point — perfect for chicken, eggs, and fish.

Reduce *(reduction)* — The process of quickly boiling down a liquid to enhance its flavor and transform its consistency without the use of a thickening agent.

Ricer *(to rice)* — A kitchen tool; a handled tool that resembles a large garlic press, with the purpose of forcing cooked fruits and root vegetables into rice-size bits, free of lumps.

Roux — Equal amounts of flour and butter (or any other fat) heated together until the flour is cooked; used for thickening sauces and soups.

Score — The process of making shallow cuts in fish or meat, usually in a diamond pattern or parallel slashes, for decoration or tenderization.

Sear — The process of quick cooking food over high heat to brown — usually the first step of a multi-step cooking process. Searing does not seal in the juices; browning it does add to the overall flavor.

Whisk — A kitchen tool; handled wire loops forming a balloon-like shape, with the purpose of adding air into foods (generally eggs or egg mixtures and sauces).

Zester — A small, hand-held kitchen tool equipped with small holes to remove the zest (colored portion) from any citrus fruit.

Coach the Cook

Apple cider can be used as a base in sauces for fowl—especially wild game birds. It is great for poaching all types of poultry or dried fruits and is delicious as a liquid in reductions. Freeze fresh cider for year 'round enjoyment; do not fill gallons to the very top.

Asparagus—To maintain freshness, keep it clean, covered and cold. Wrap stem ends in moist paper towels or stand upright in a few inches of water. Asparagus should be cooked and eaten as soon as possible as it will only keep for a few days in the refrigerator.

Cauliflower should not be cooked in aluminum or cast iron—these metals will change the color of the cauliflower. To keep it perfectly white, add lemon or lemon juice to the water.

Chiles can cause distress to the face and eyes if contact is made. The heat of the capsicum remains on hands, fingers and fingernails for long periods of time. Wear rubber or surgical gloves when seeding and deveining chiles.

Cleaning vegetables—Use a clean plastic pot scrubber or a vegetable brush.

Condiments can be easily enhanced. Transform traditional ketchup and mustard by adding herbs, spices and extracts.

Cranberries cooked in cranberry juice create a more intense flavor. When cooking them for cranberry sauce, add sugar after the berries have popped to eliminate any toughness of the skins.

Dental floss (unflavored) makes an excellent tress for poultry, or for cutting cheesecake clean.

Edible flowers add eye appeal and sometimes a spicy flavor to foods. Not all garden flowers are edible, so carefully check to make sure they are not poisonous and that they are bug and pesticide free. Organically grown flowers are the safest bet since flowers purchased from a florist or a specialty store are usually sprayed with toxins. Use blossoms and petals of flowers, not leaves and stems (Nasturtium leaves are an exception). Use only the petals of large flowers or small flowers whole. Edible Flowers: Anise Hyssop flowers, Arugula flowers, Basil (sweet) flowers, Borage, Calendula, Carnation, Chamomile, Chervil flowers, Chive flowers, Dandelion, Day Lily, Dill flowers, Lavender, Marigolds, Mustards, Mint flowers, Nasturtiums, Pansies (only in small amounts), Rose petals, Rosemary flowers, Sage flowers, Snapdragons, Squash blossoms, Thyme flowers and Violets.

Grease can be removed from soups and sauces by cooling down, refrigerating, then lightly placing a paper towel on top to collect the grease. It may also be removed by spooning off.

Infuse (flavor) olive or vegetable oil with herbs, garlic or spices. Then, for a flavor boost, sauté vegetables, fish or poultry in the flavored oil.

Juicing a lemon or lime — Prior to squeezing, press fruit firmly and roll it on a hard surface. To squeeze drop by drop, prick a small hole in the skin.

Marinate meat, fish and poultry in nonreactive containers (glass, porcelain or enamel) in the refrigerator. For food safety, do not marinate on the kitchen counter.

Meat can be sliced thin to paper-thin by partially freezing the meat prior to slicing.

Nuts can be deadly to someone who is allergic to them. Make sure whenever serving, or giving nuts as a gift, the recipient has no related allergies. If serving nuts, make sure they are fresh — they should not rattle in their shells.

Pesto can be frozen for later use. To use for pasta sauce, freeze in 1 to 1 1/2 cup containers. For flavoring in soups, stews and sauces, freeze in ice cube trays.

Plastic wrap will cling better if the rim of the container is moist.

Prepare all raw meat on a clean kitchen surface. Make sure the cutting board is cleaned with bleach water (one teaspoon of bleach to a quart of very hot water). After meat preparation, re-clean cutting board with bleach water to avoid cross-contamination.

Thaw frozen foods in the refrigerator, not at room temperature. Never leave raw food exposed at room temperature for more than one hour. To eliminate bacteria concerns, do not refreeze thawed foods.

Thicken soups and stews with quick-cooking oats — or grated, instant, or leftover mashed potatoes.

"When in Doubt — Throw it Out" — If there is any question to freshness of food (refrigerated or frozen), or foods with strange odors or appearances, discard them. Never risk food-borne illness.

Wild mushrooms should always be cooked before eating; never eat them raw. To reconstitute dried mushrooms, soak in warm water for 20-30 minutes, or overnight in cold water. Use the strained mushroom  water in stocks or recipes. All mushrooms, wild or cultivated, pair well with nutmeg, butter, cream and a variety of herbs.

Discover More Secrets...

Now secret recipes from the best restaurants in other great cities can be yours.

Don't delay! Inventory is limited and all orders are subject to availability.

Secrets
RESTAURANT

Only $20 Each

Collection Series: 1999 Edition

Great for Gifts!

CALIFORNIA		**MASSACHUSETTS**		**NEW YORK**	
Fresno/Central Valley	99RS86	Boston	99RS30	Albany/Capital District	99RS60
San Francisco Bay		**MARYLAND**		Mid Hudson Valley	99RST8
Area/Wine Country	99RS55	Greater Baltimore	99RS24	**OHIO**	
Orange County	99RS14	**MICHIGAN**		Greater Cincinnati	99RS02
Sacramento/Gold Country	99RS42	Detroit	99RS01	**OREGON**	
San Diego	99RS17	Grand Rapids	99RSP2	Portland	99RS29
CONNECTICUT		**MINNESOTA**		**PENNSYLVANIA**	
Northern Connecticut	99RS46	Twin Cities	99RST3	South Central	
DISTRICT OF COLUMBIA		**MISSOURI**		Pennsylvania	99RS72
Greater Washington, DC	99RS22	Kansas City	99RS20	**WASHINGTON**	
FLORIDA		St. Louis	99RS13	Seattle	99RS23
South Florida	99RS35	**NEW JERSEY**		**WISCONSIN**	
ILLINOIS		Central New Jersey	99RS48	Appleton/Green Bay	99RS77
Chicago	99RS08	Northern New Jersey	99RS26	Milwaukee	99RS32
				PLUS	
				Puerto Rico	99RS1T

Ordering is Easy!!!

Simply call 1-800-374-4464 to order other editions. Price includes first class shipping and handling.

Support local fund-raisers by purchasing local editions from them when possible.

EE91